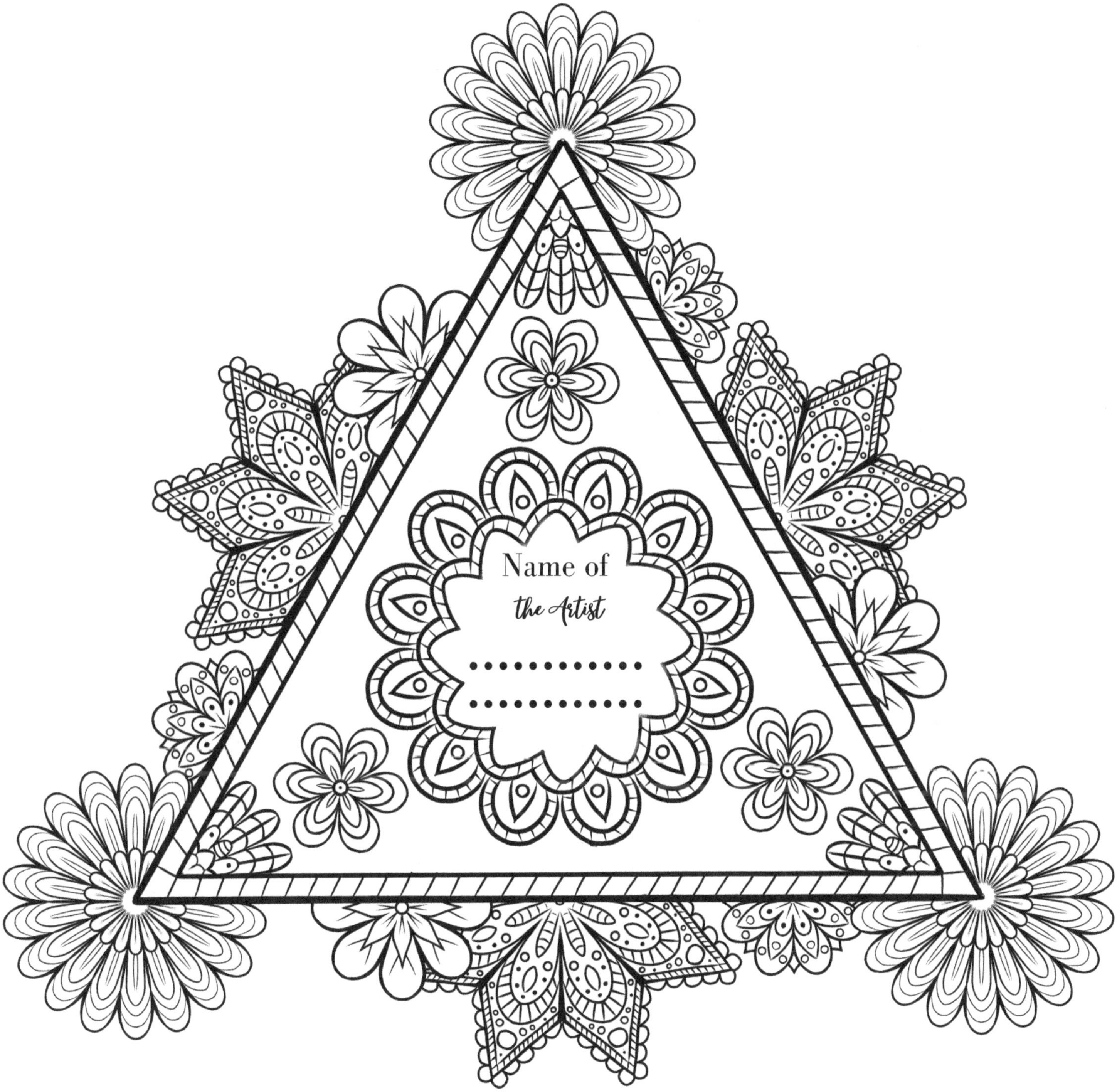

Name of
the Artist

· · · · · · · · · · · ·

· · · · · · · · · · · ·

Color Test Page

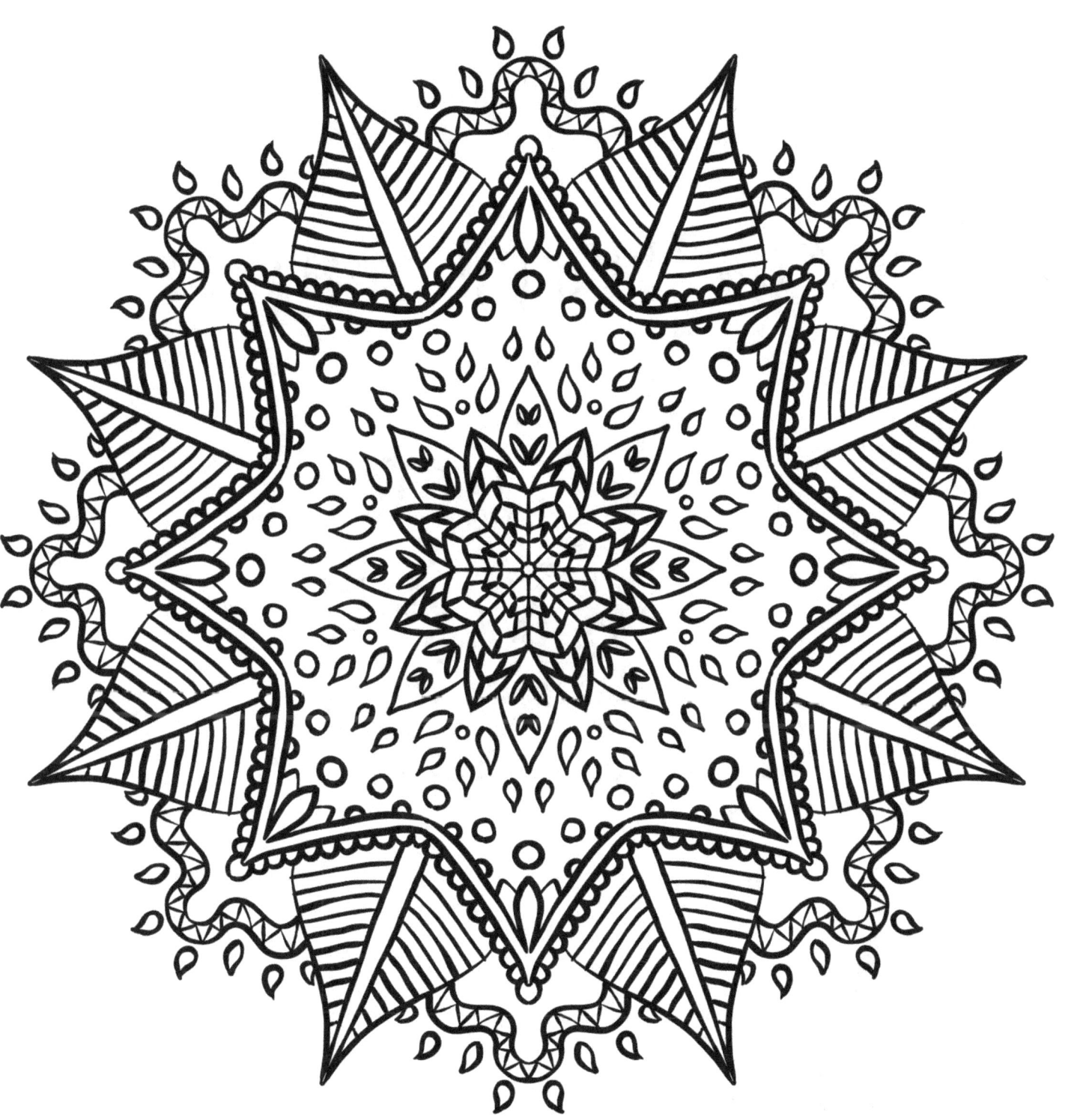

Bleed Through Barrier

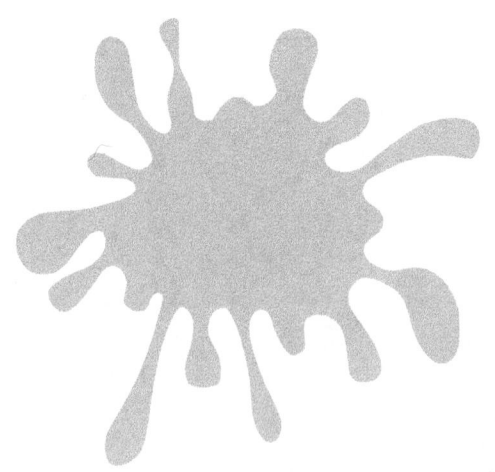

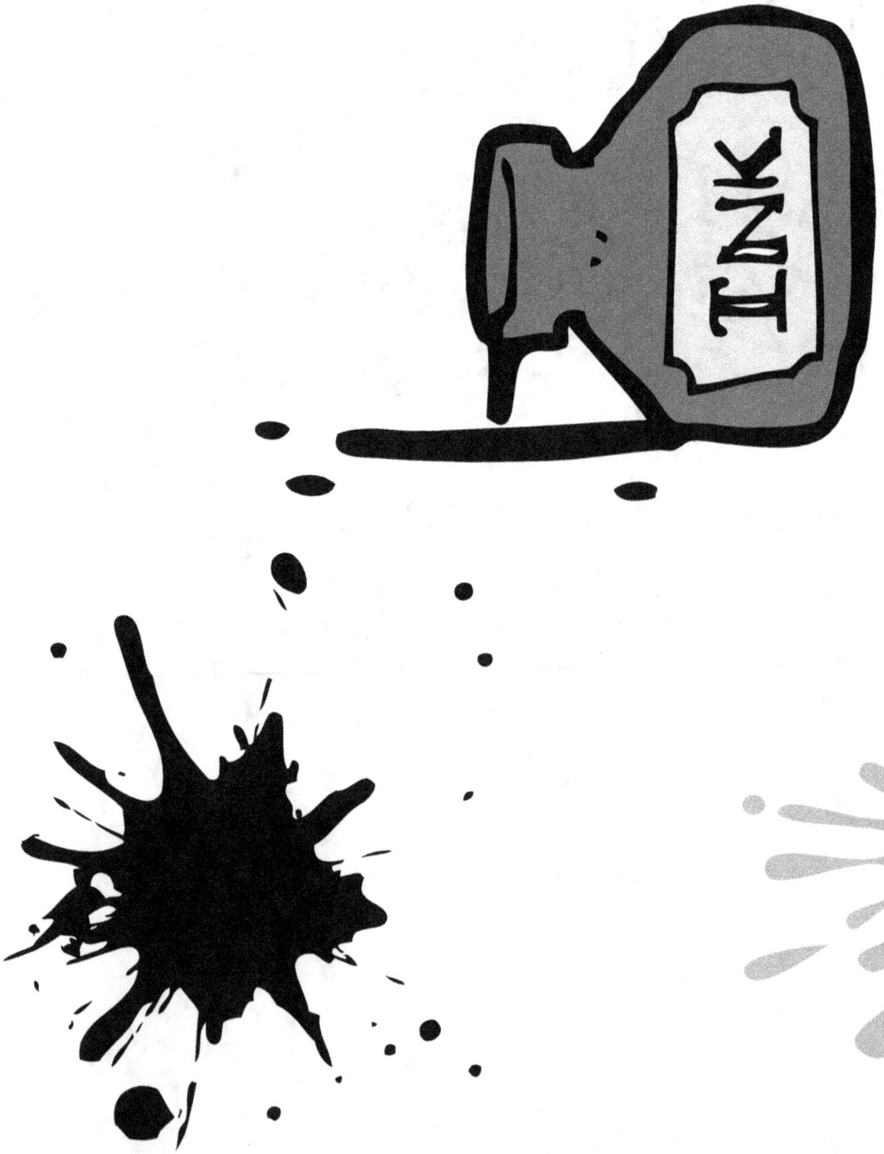

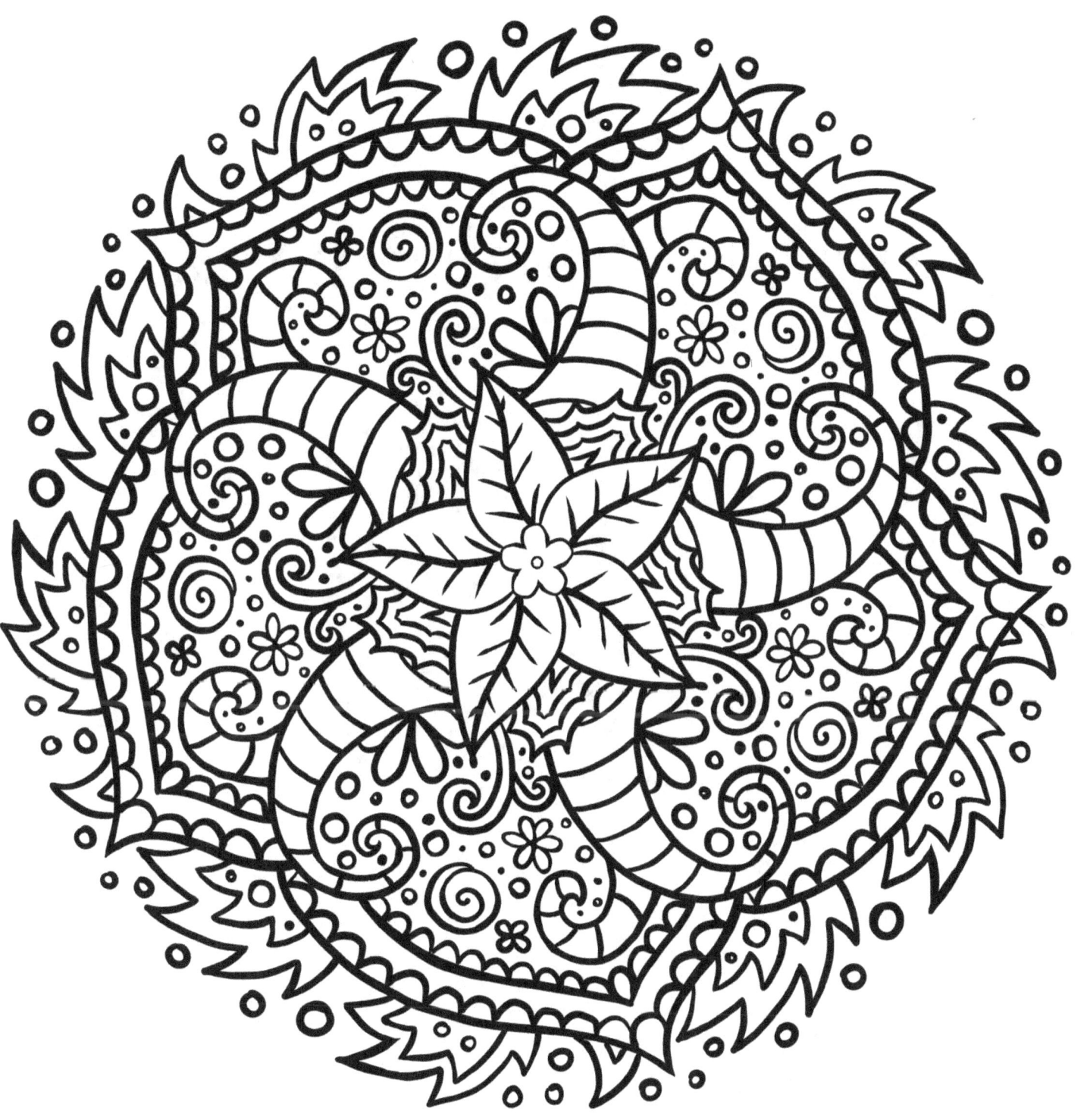

Bleed Through Barrier

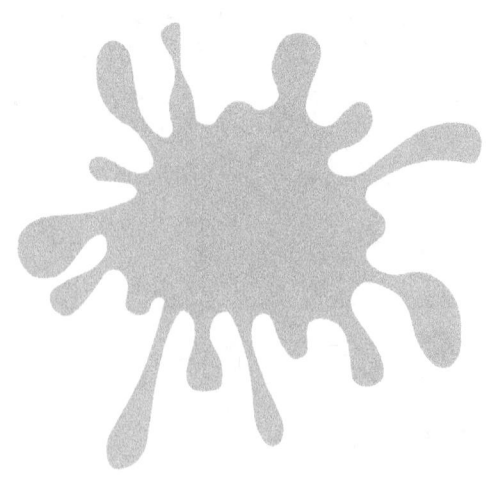

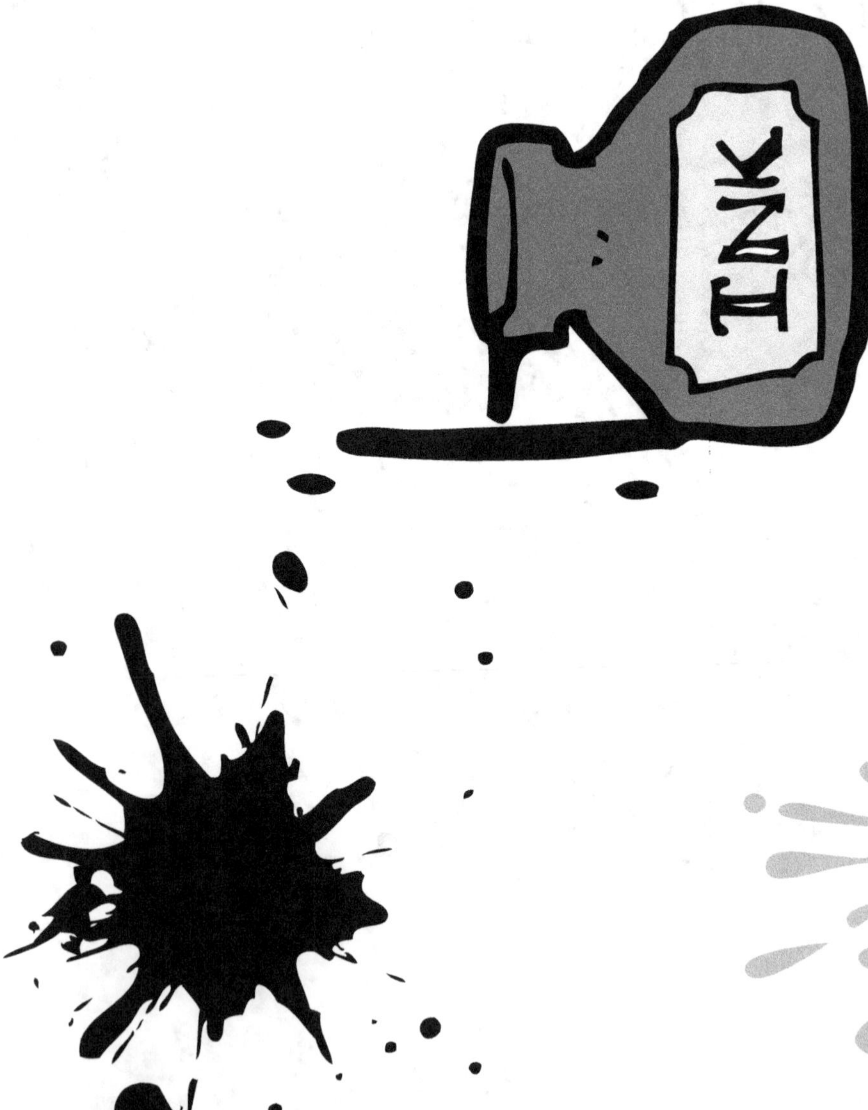

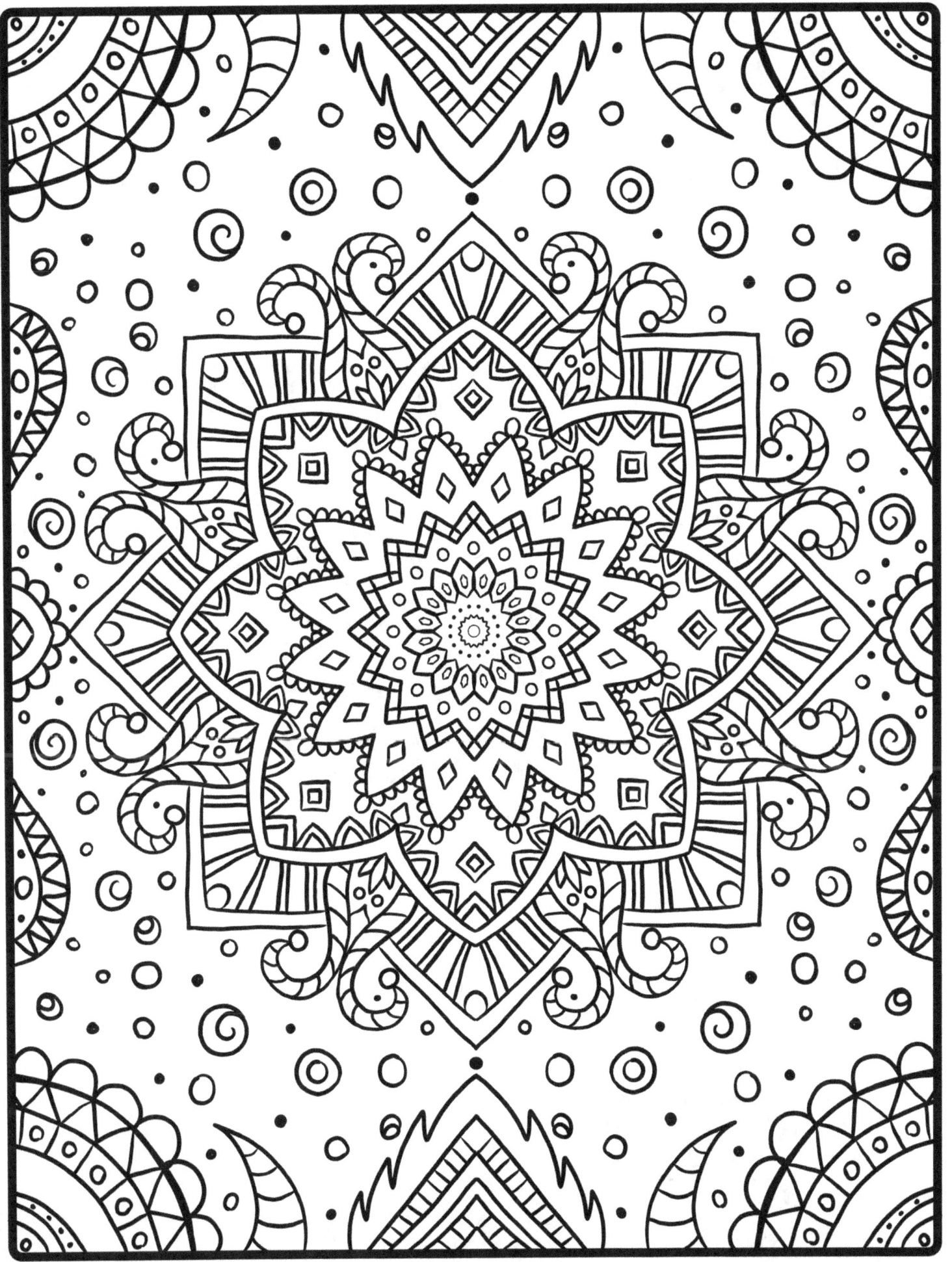

Bleed Through Barrier

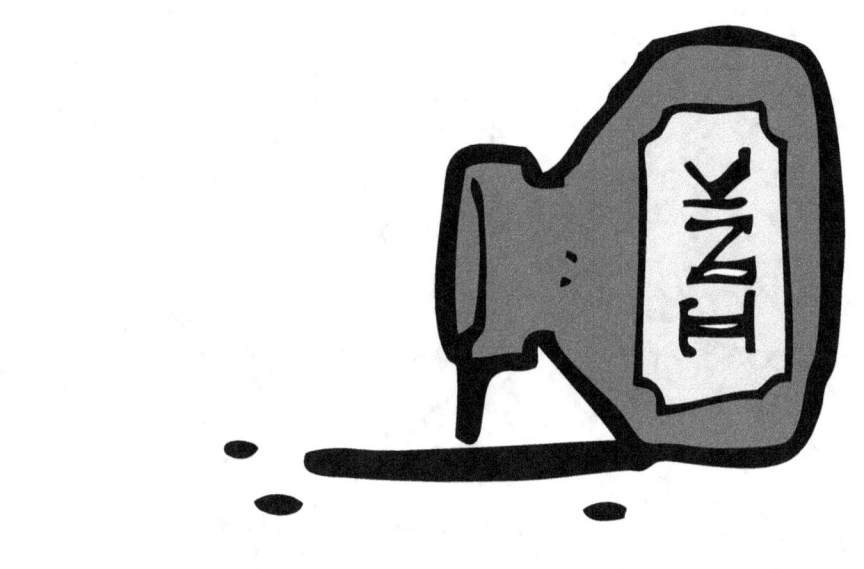

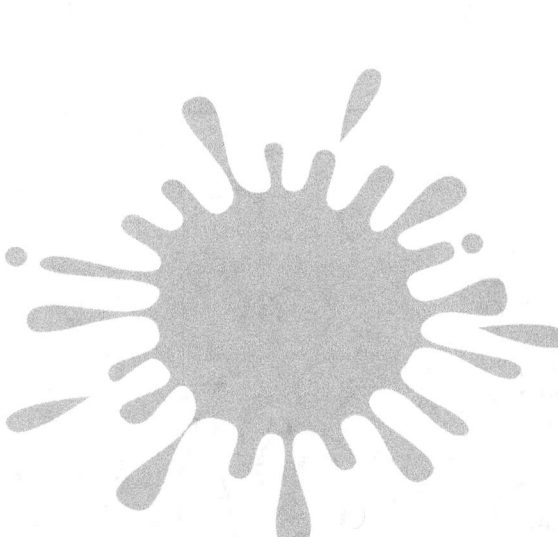

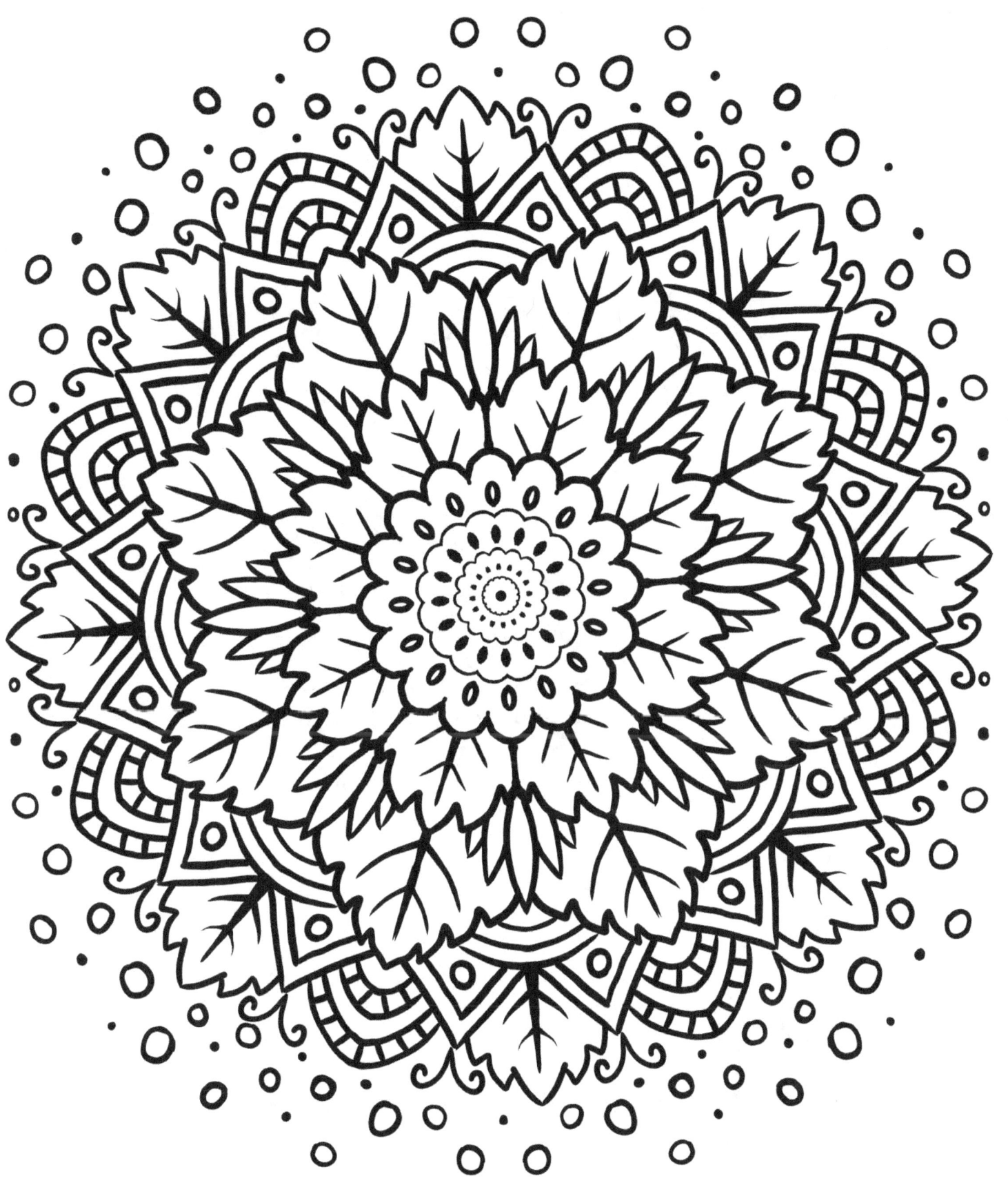

Bleed Through Barrier

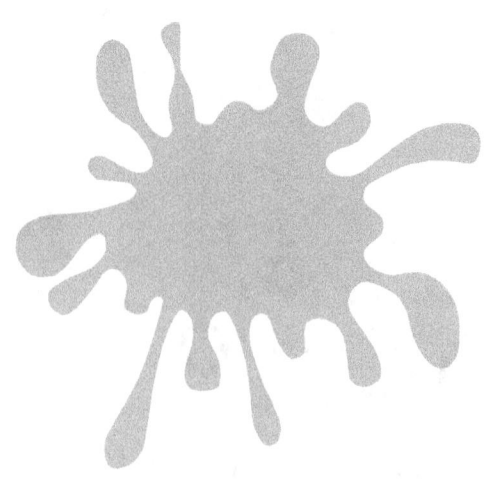

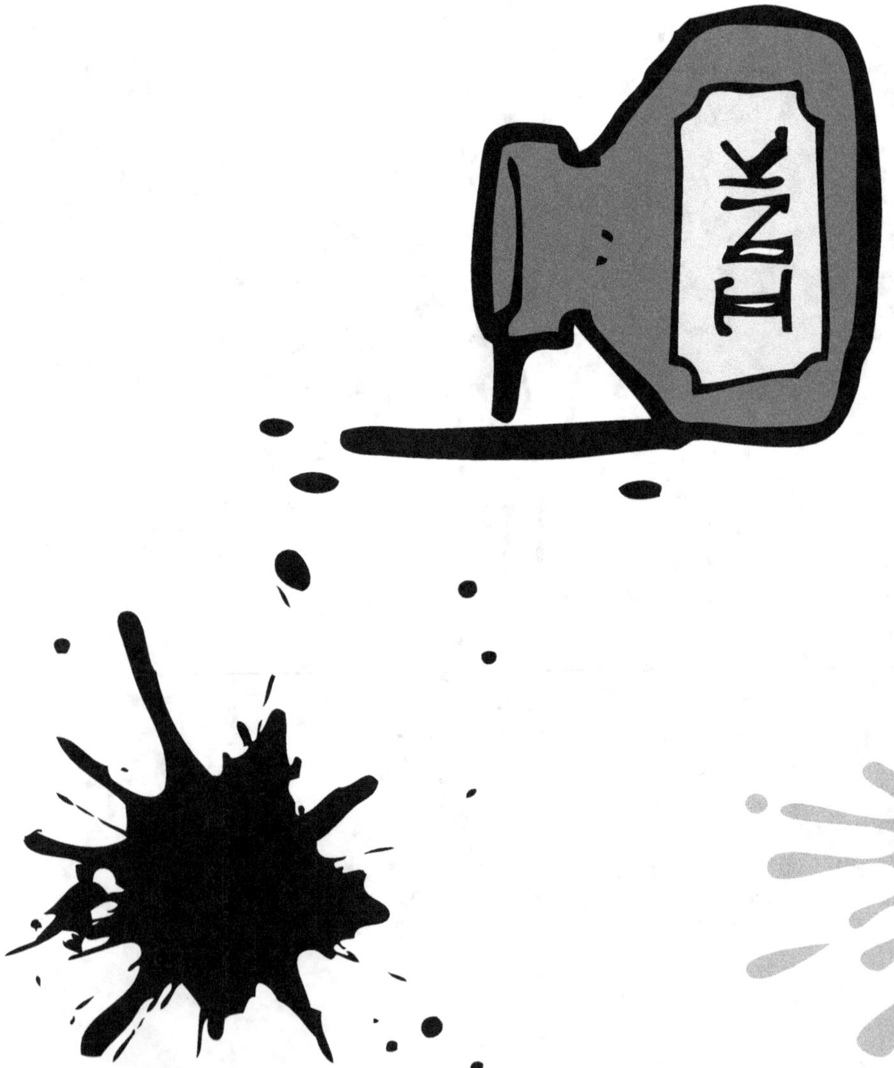

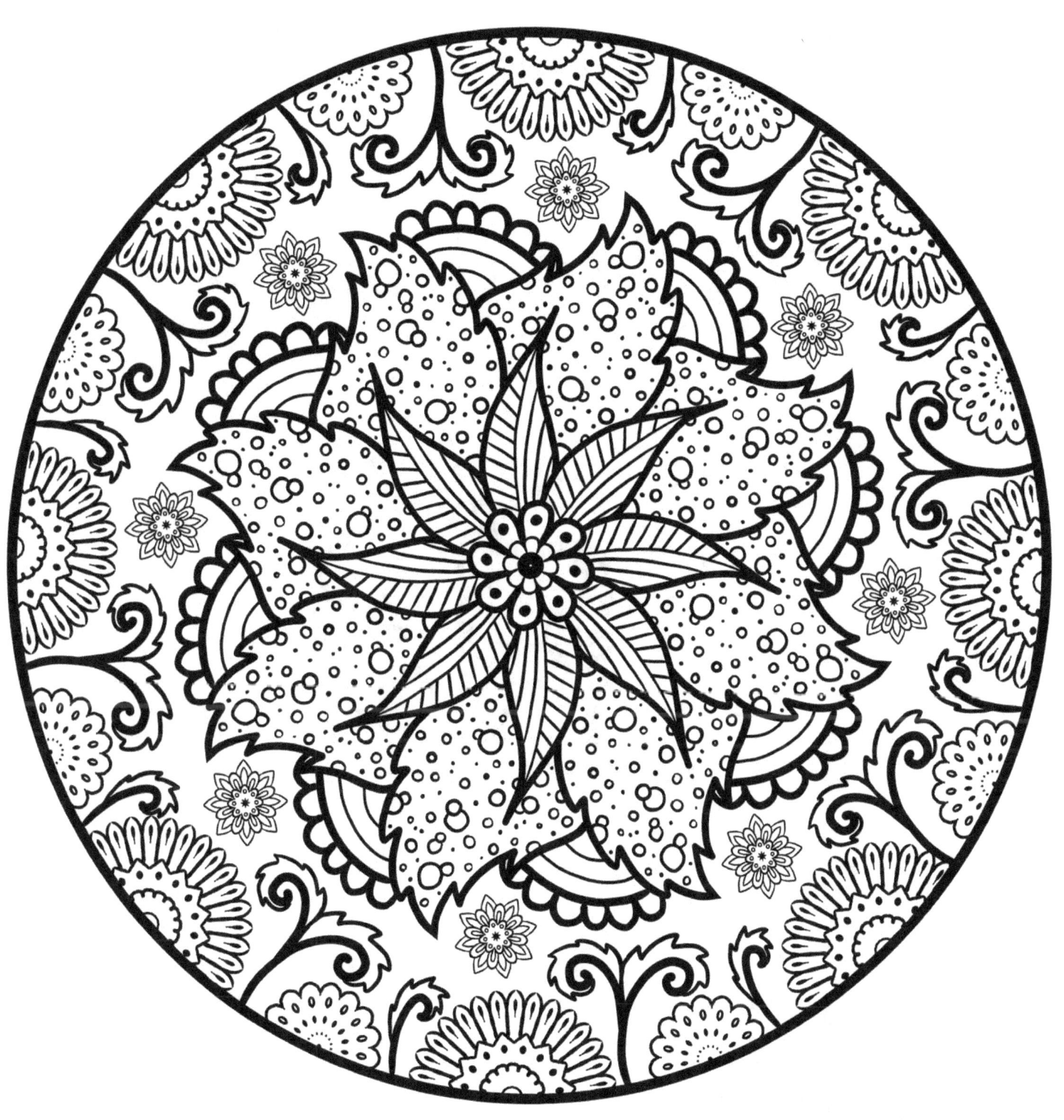

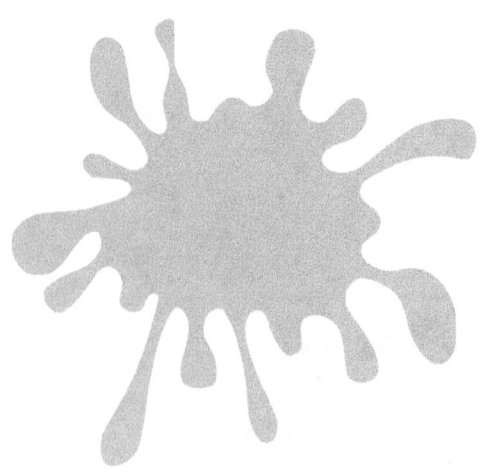

Bleed Through Barrier

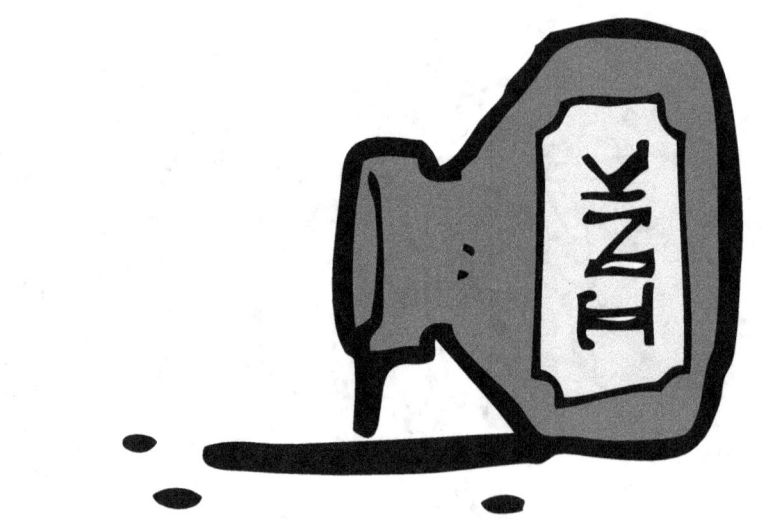

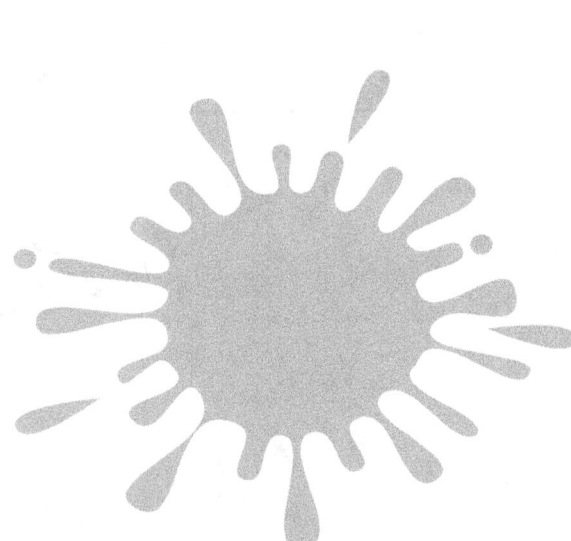

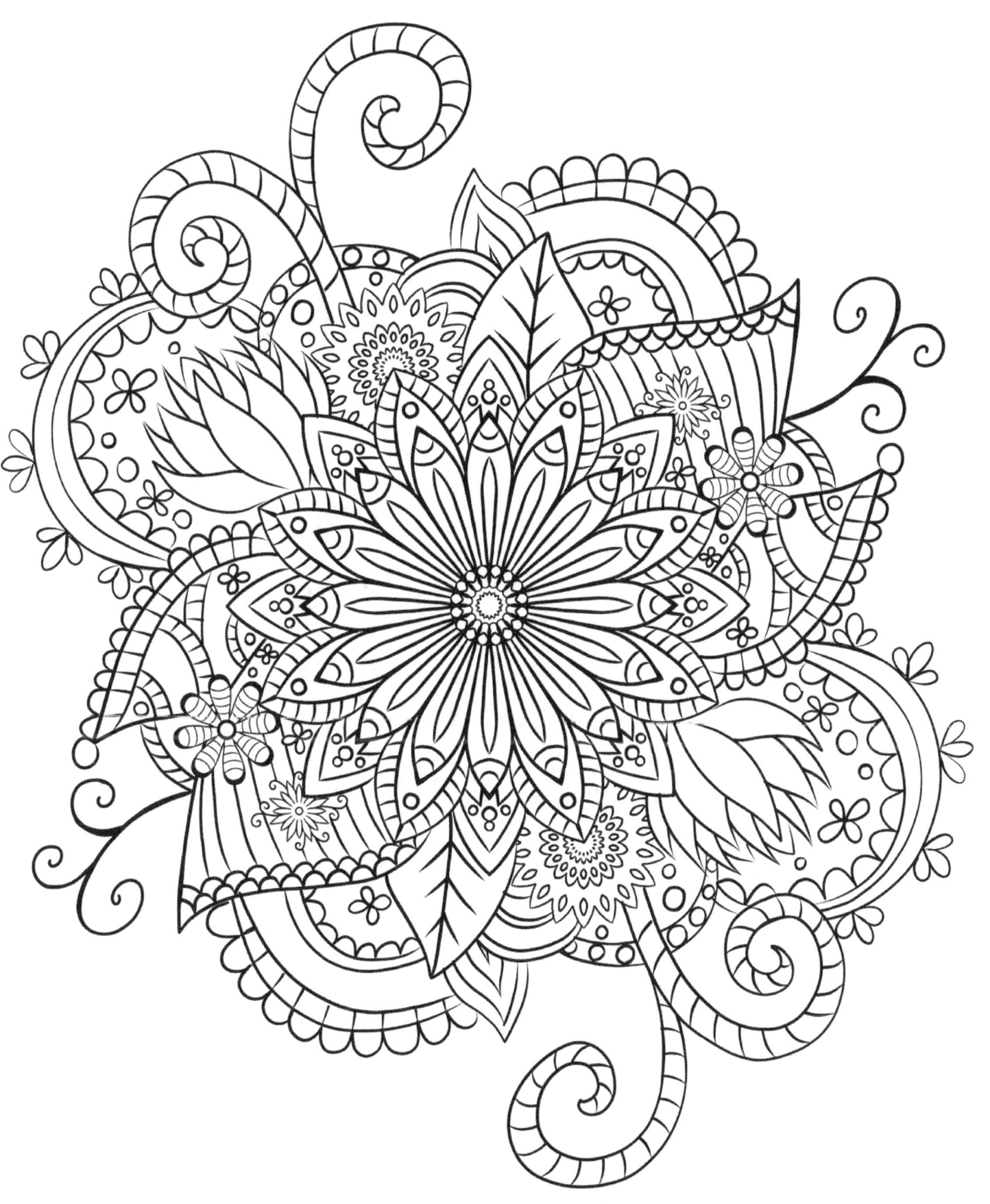

Bleed Through Barrier

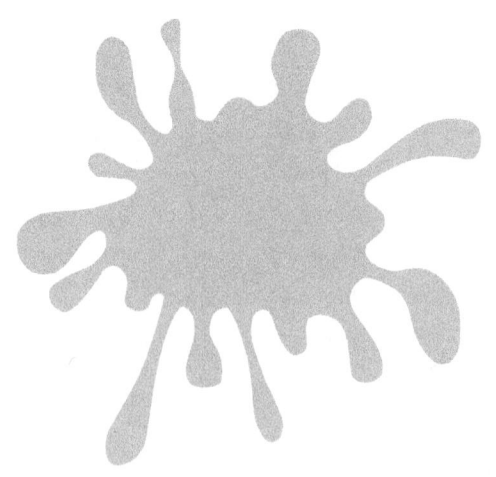

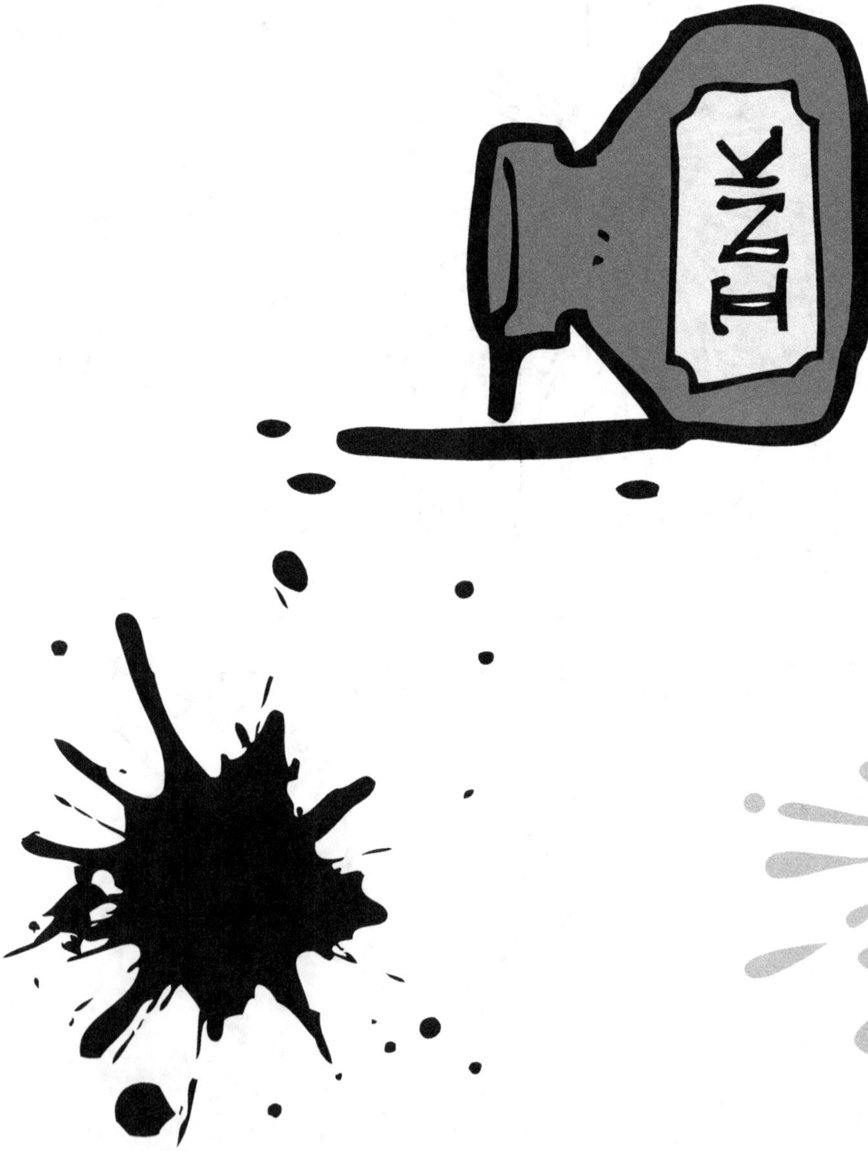

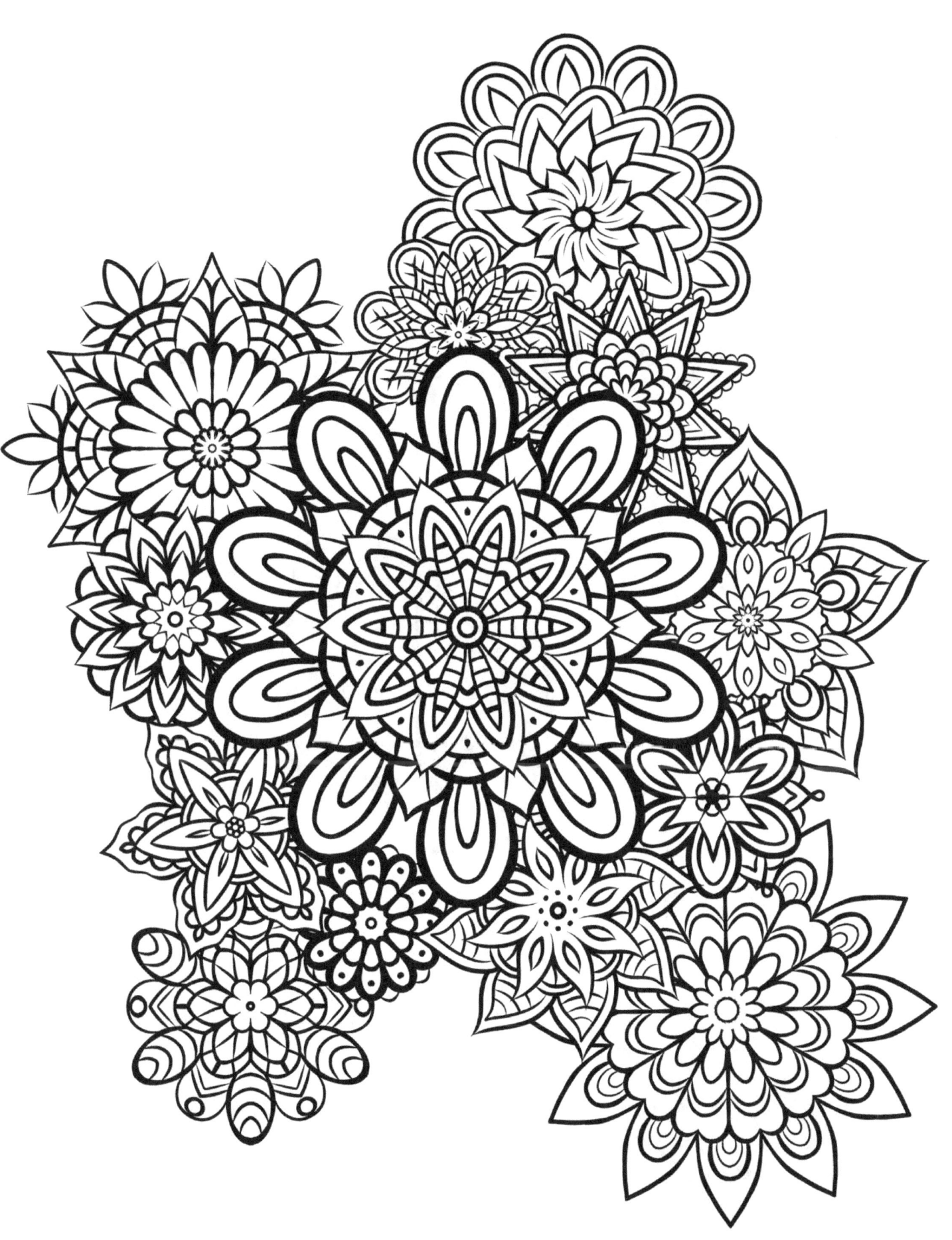

Bleed Through Barrier

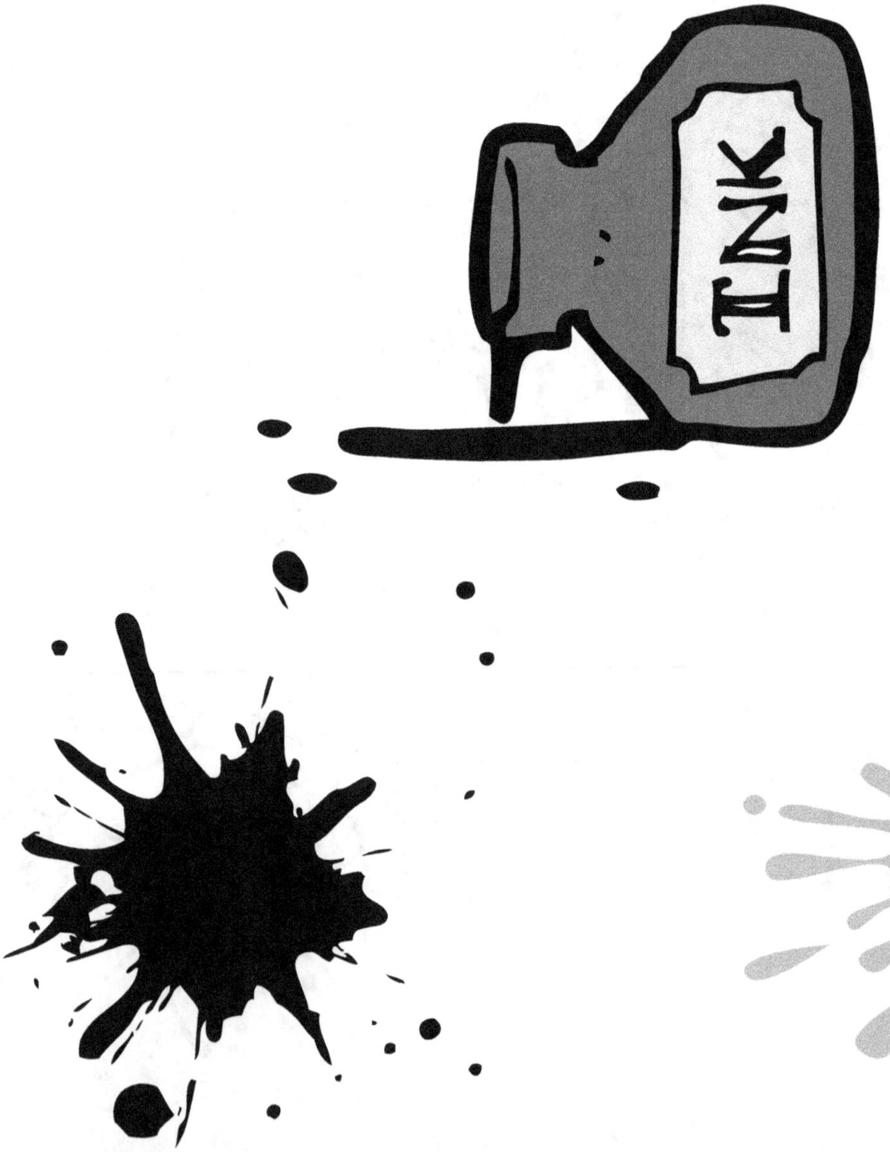

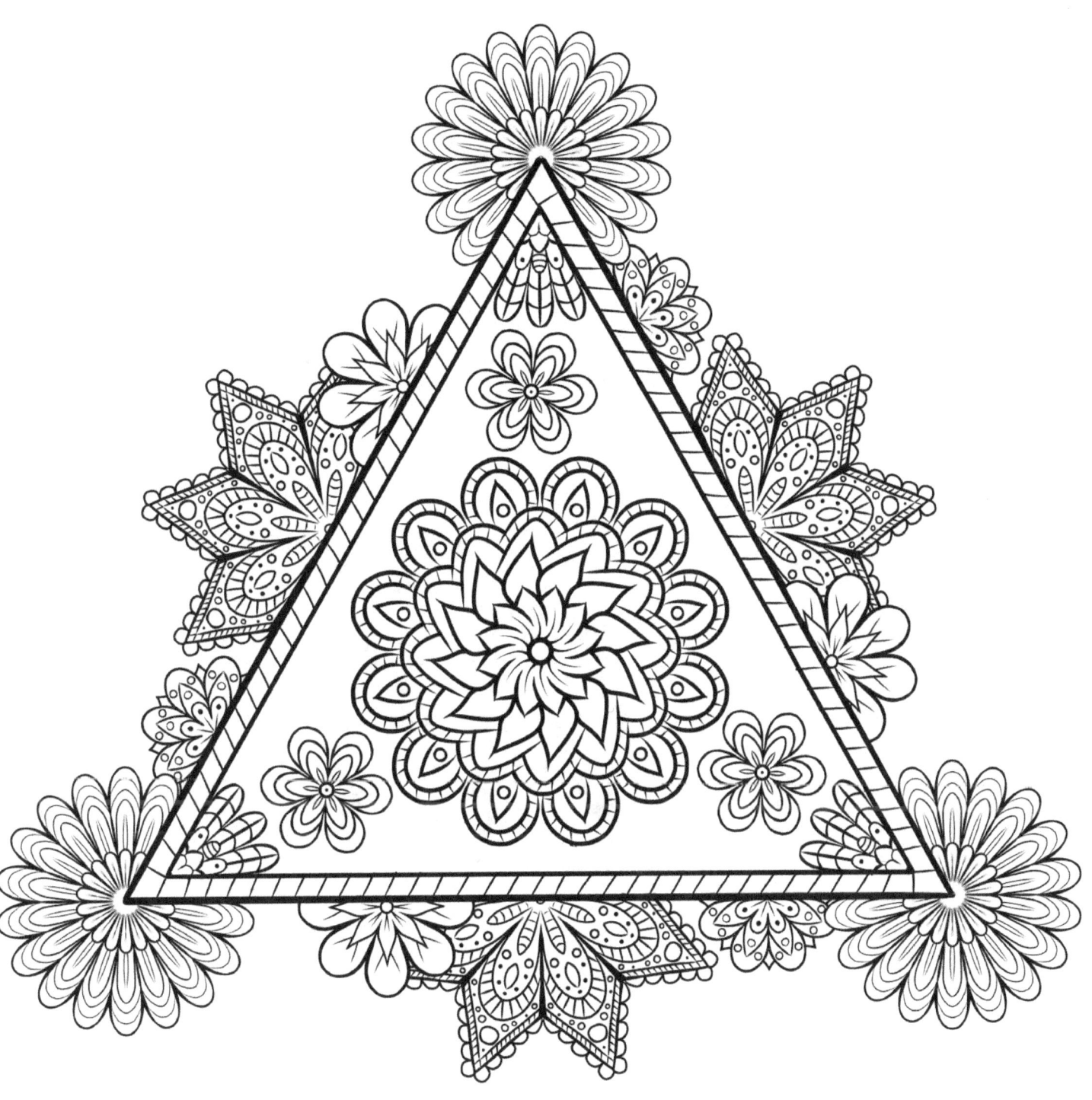

Bleed Through Barrier

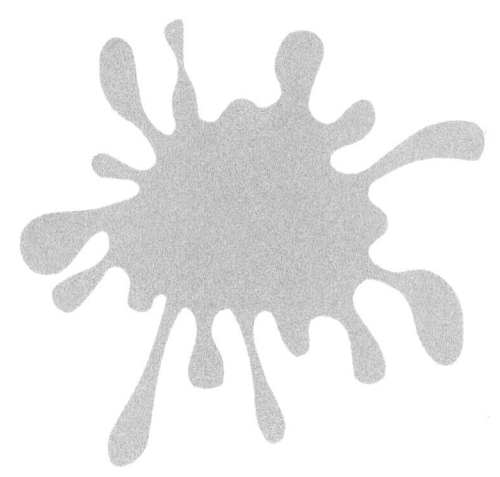

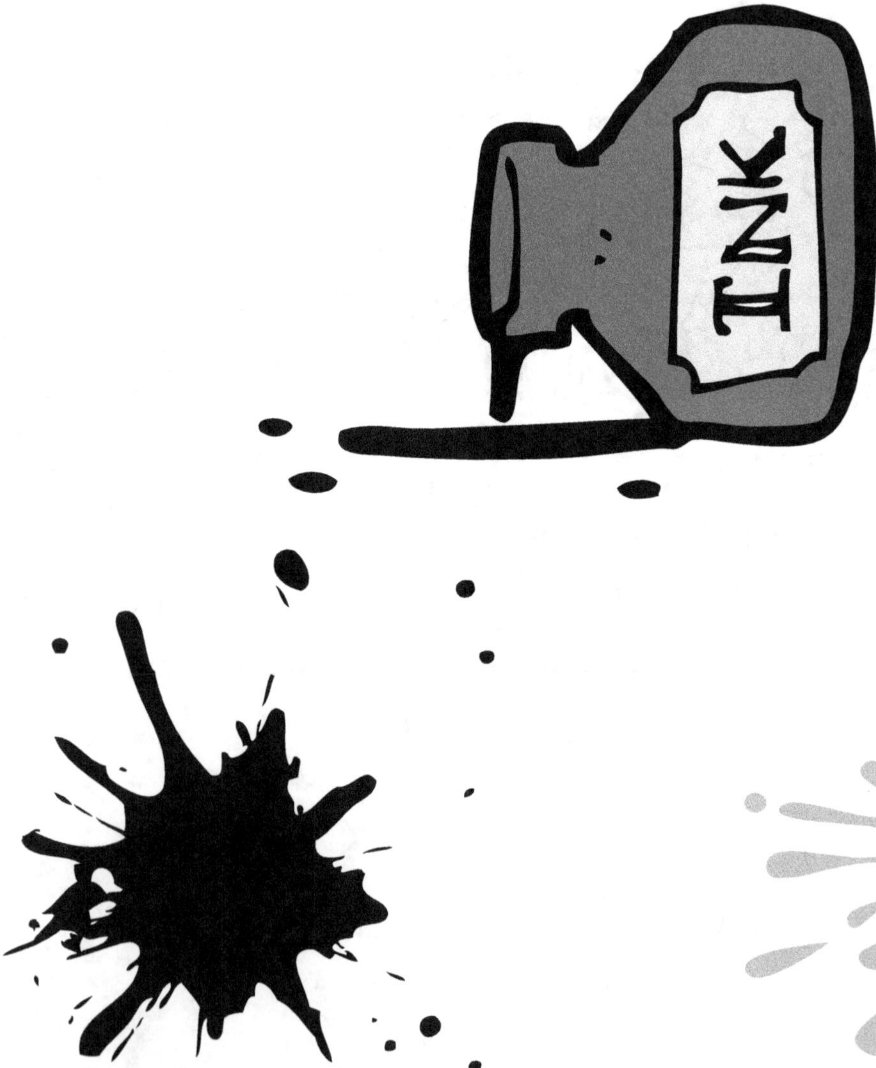

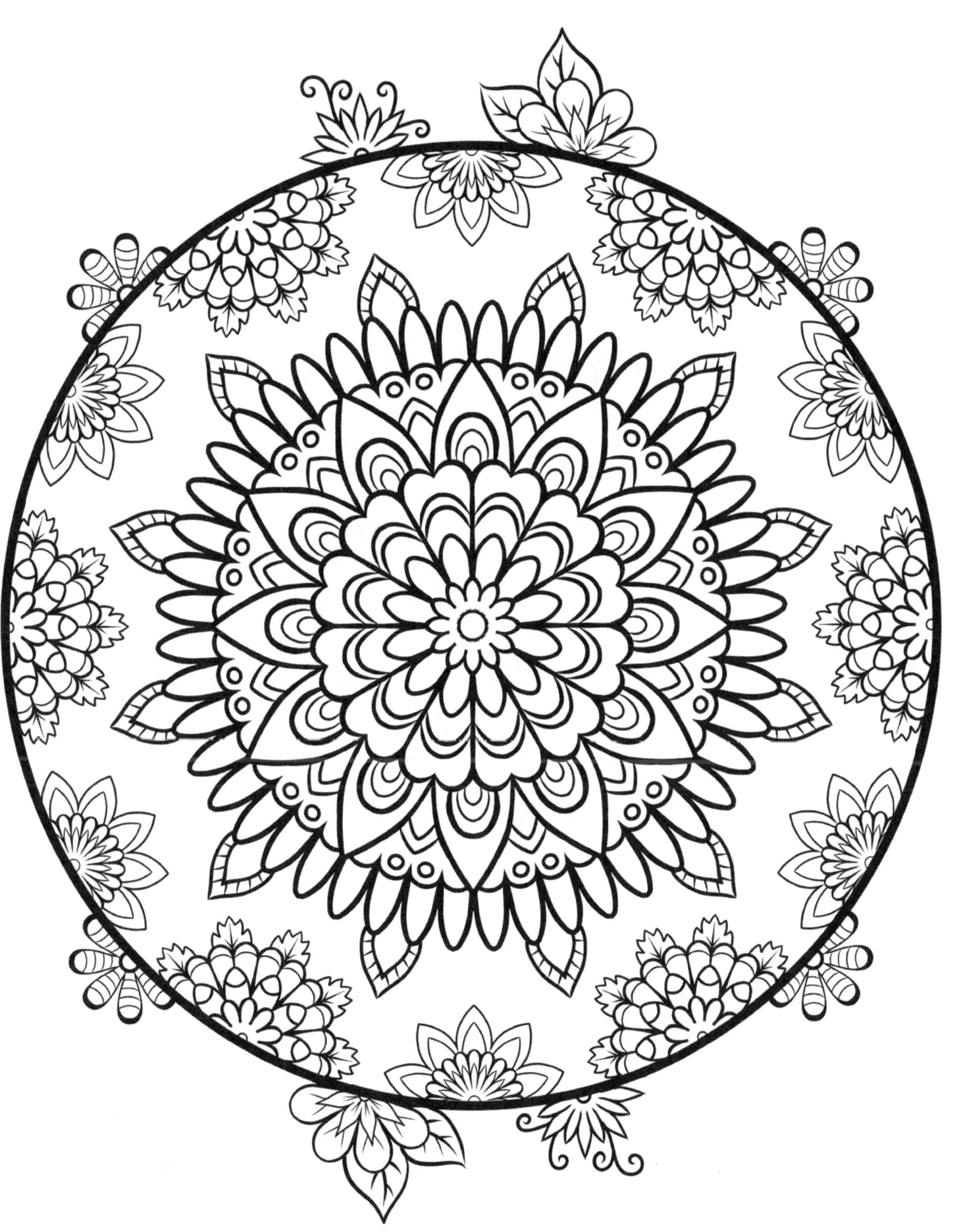

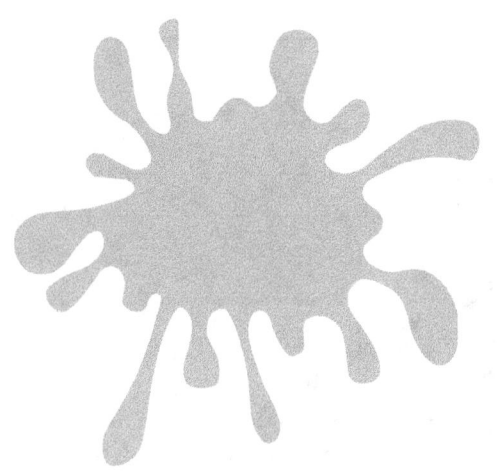

Bleed Through Barrier

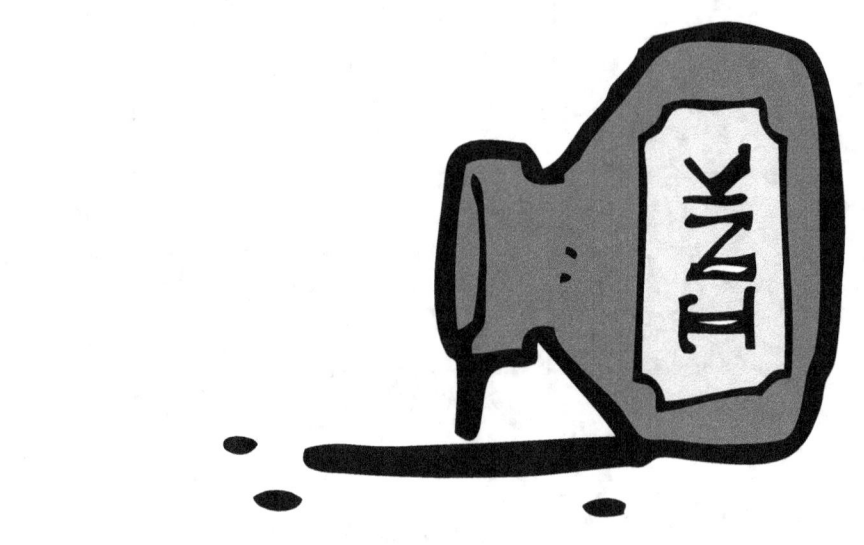

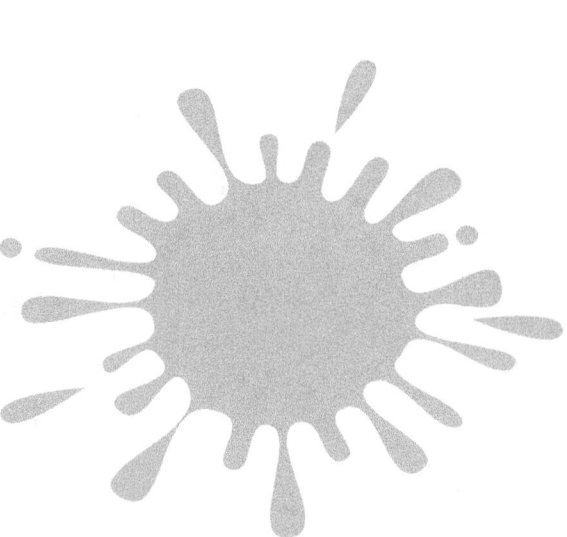

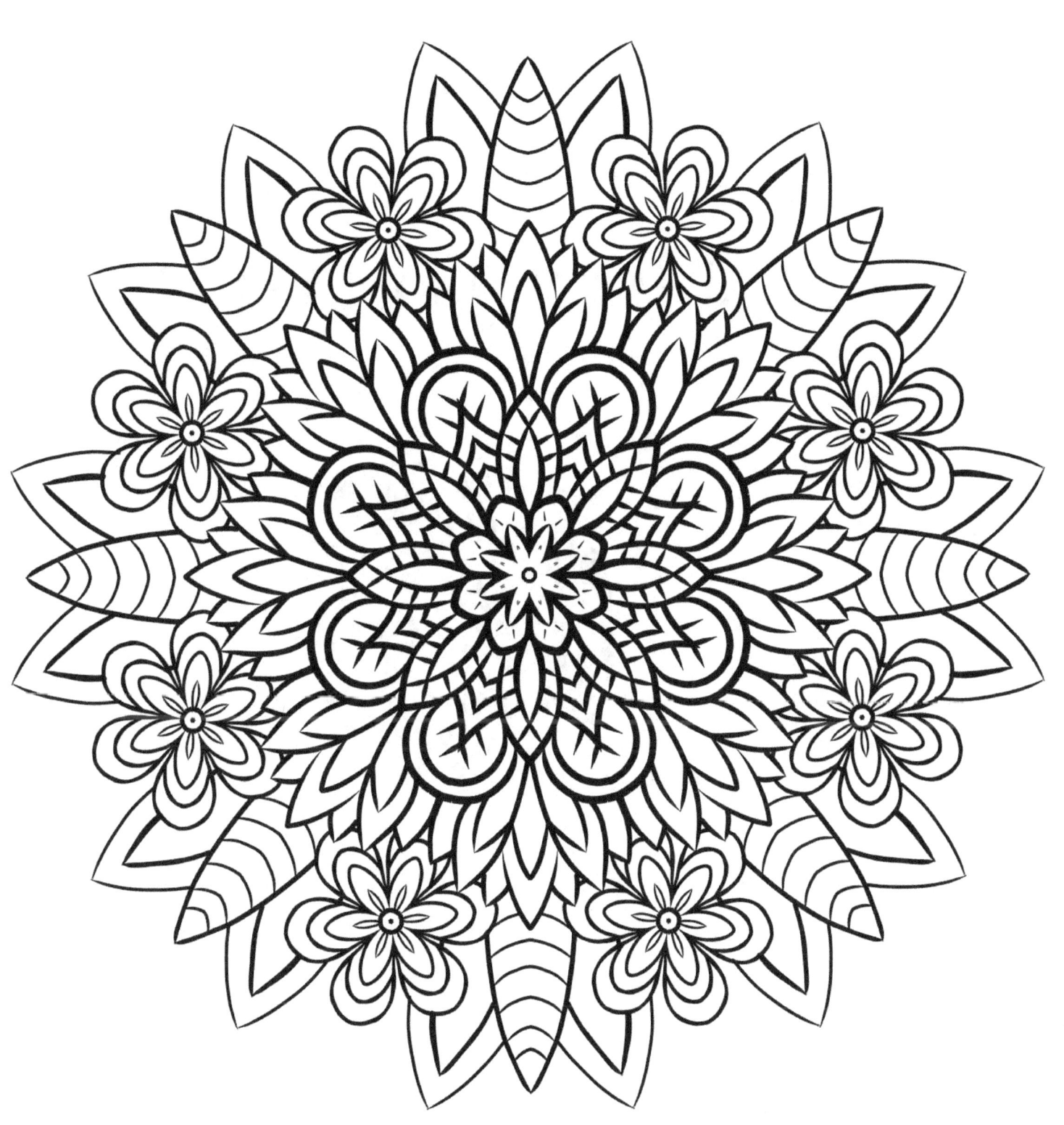

Bleed Through Barrier

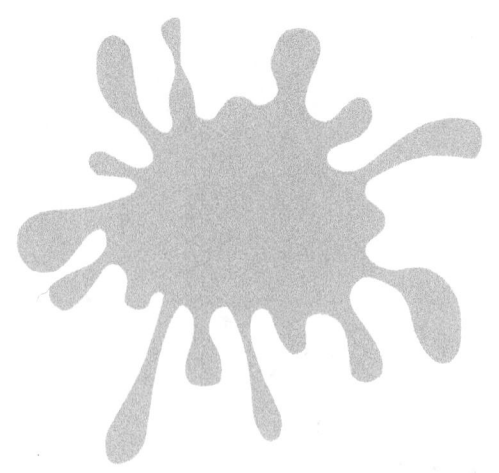

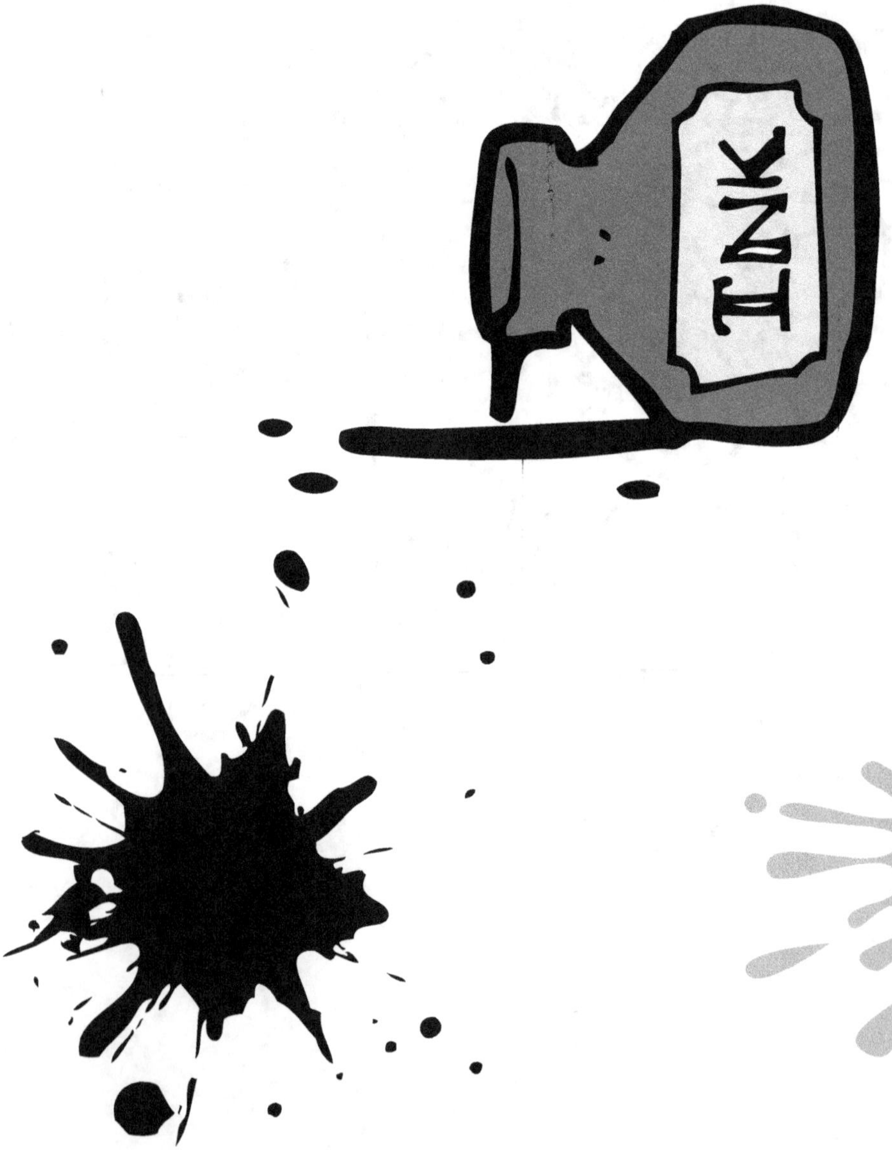

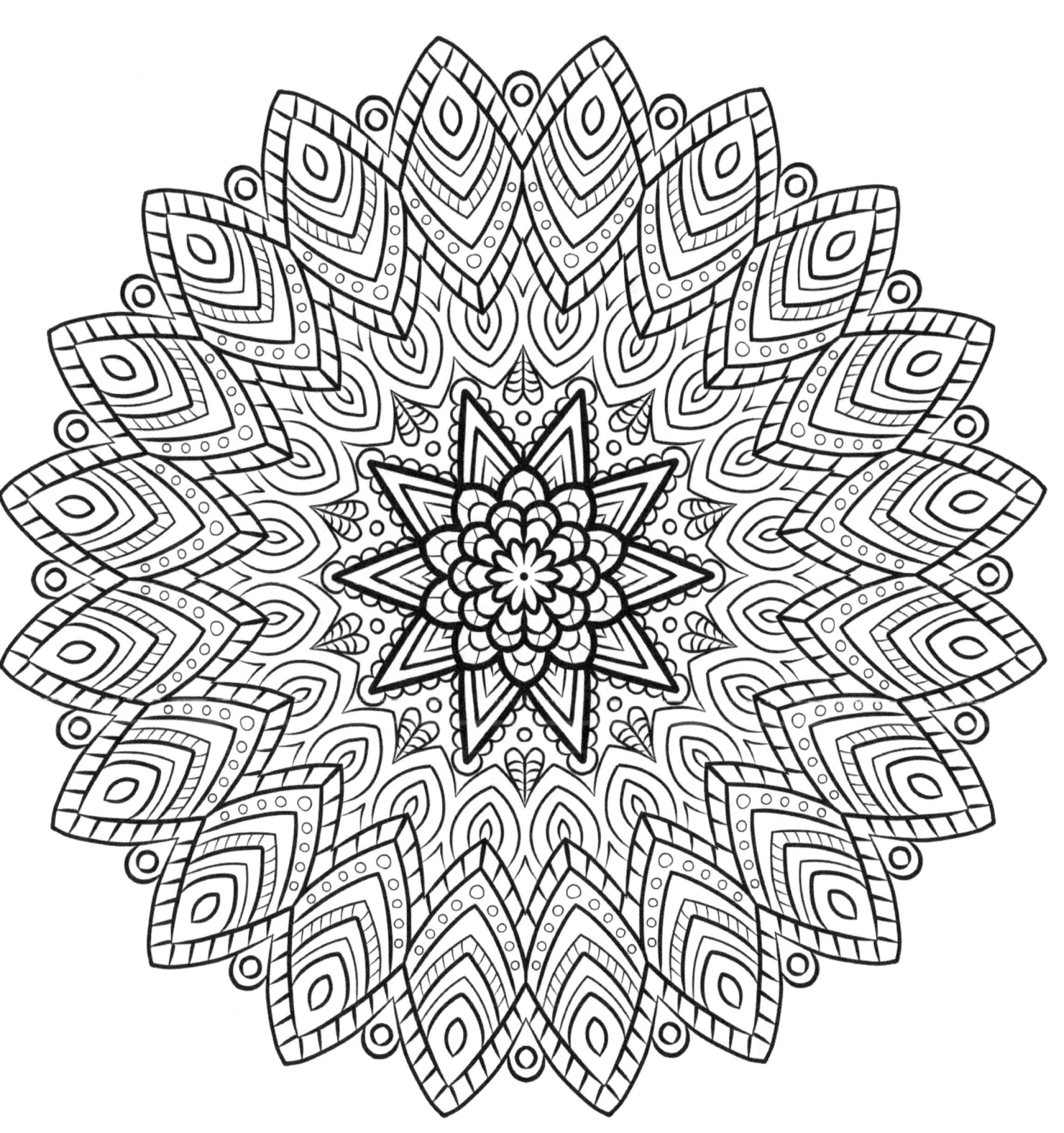

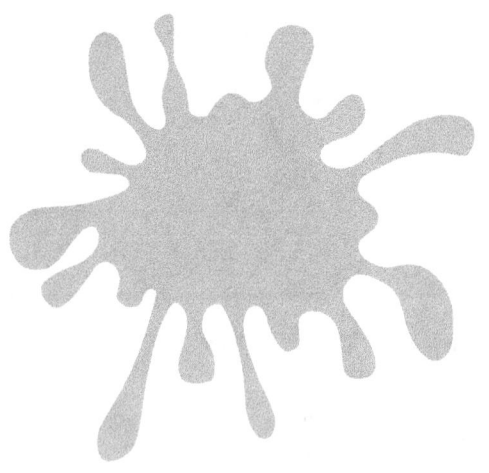

Bleed Through Barrier

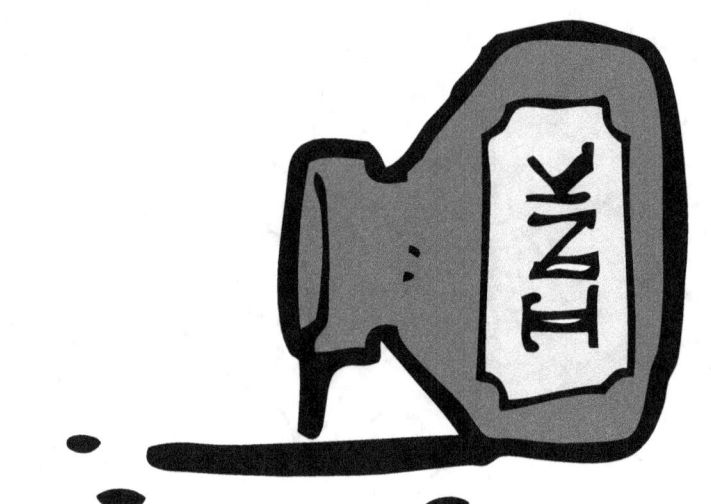

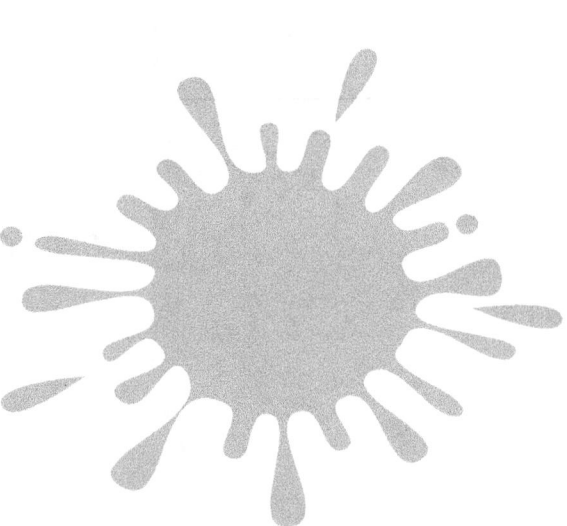

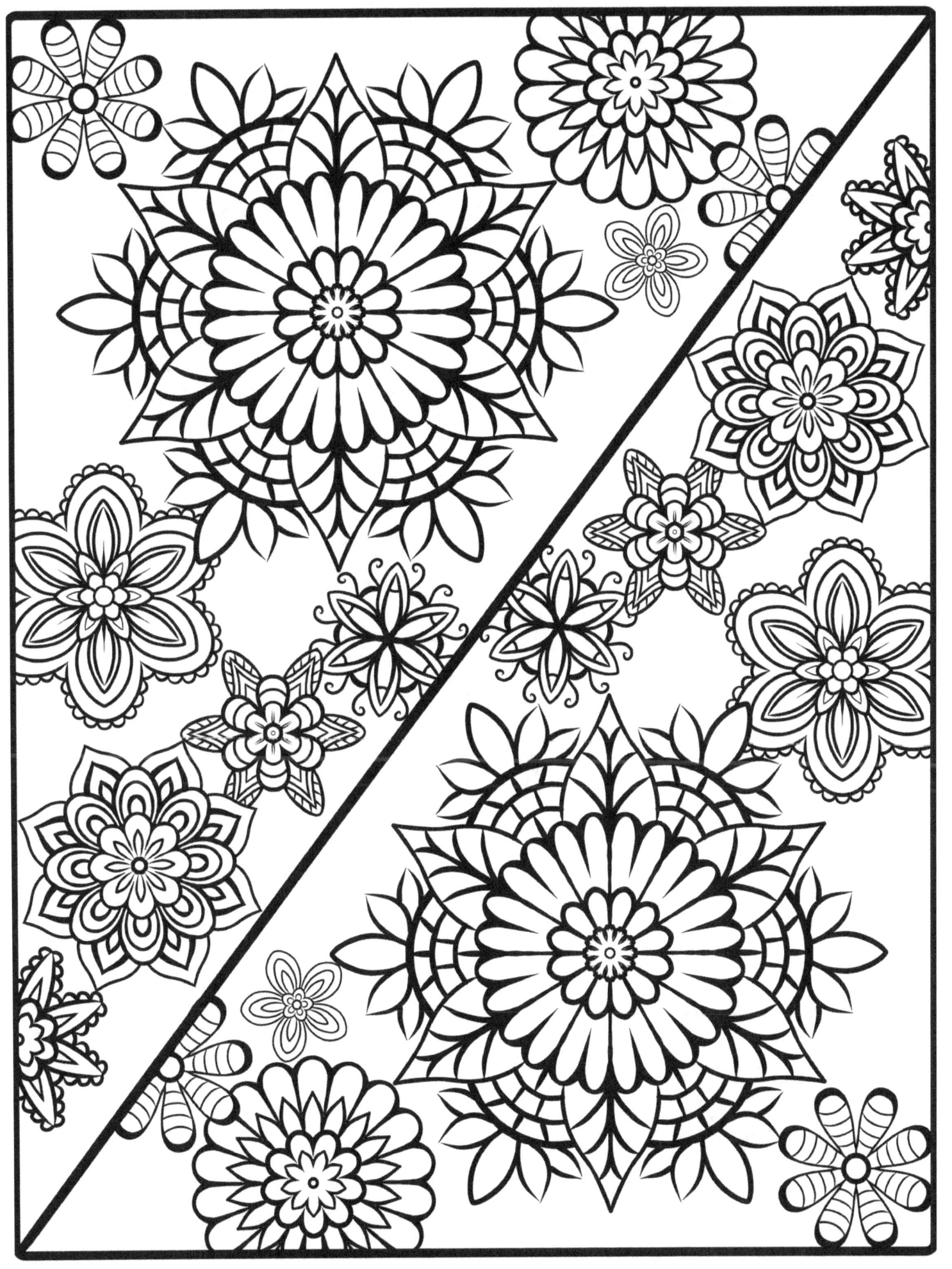

Bleed Through Barrier

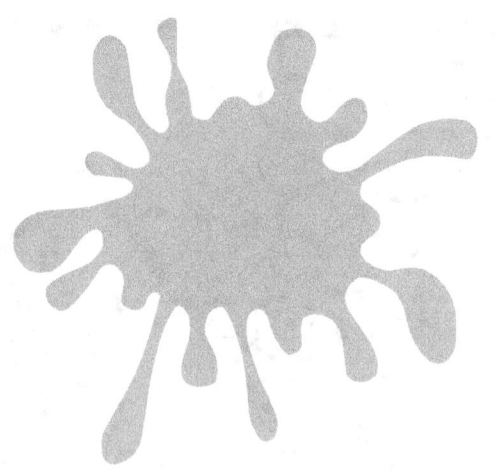

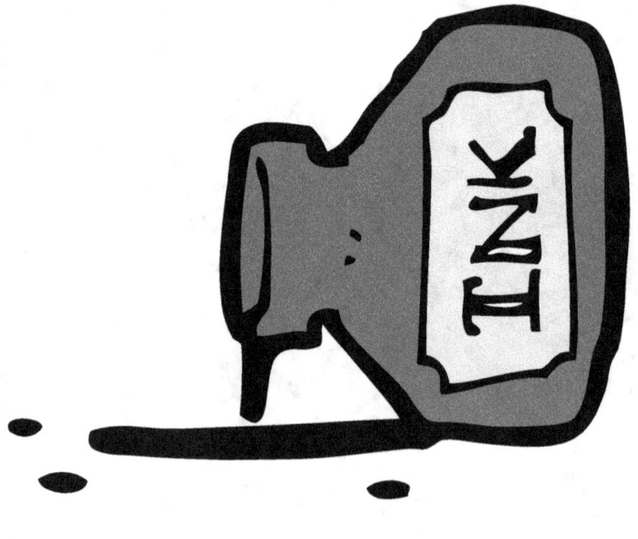

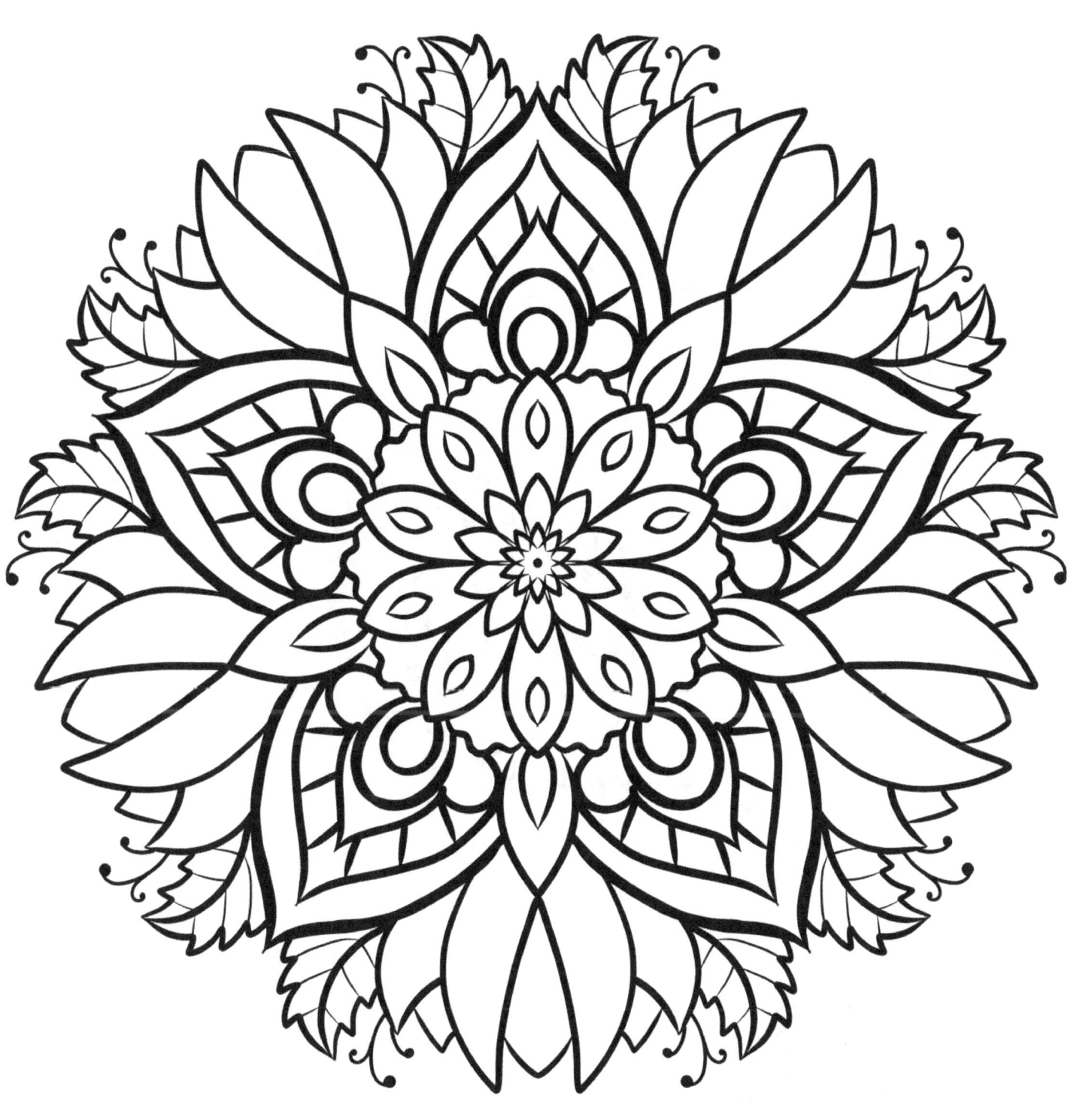

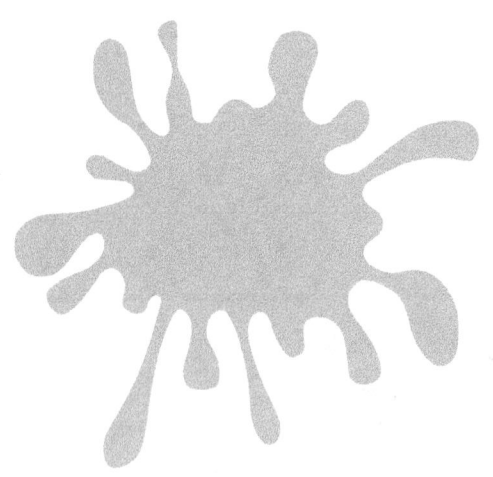

Bleed Through Barrier

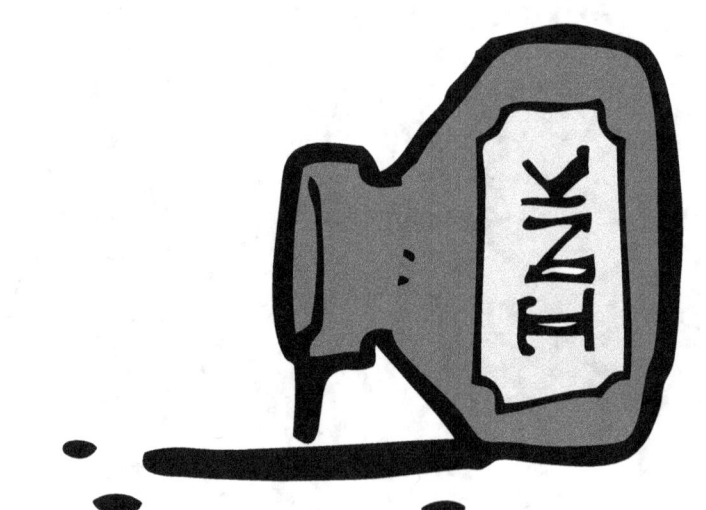

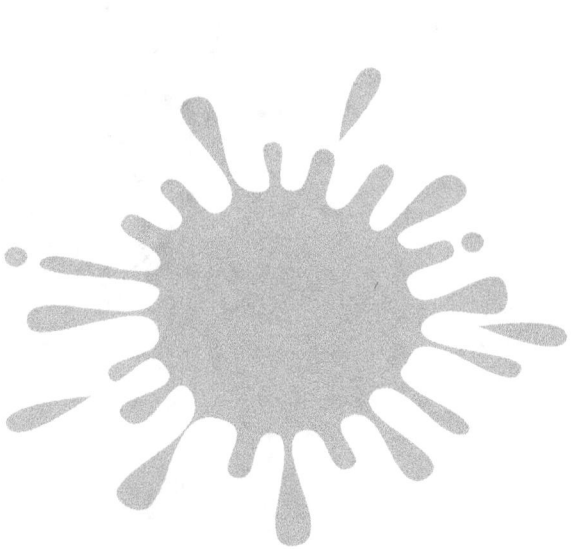

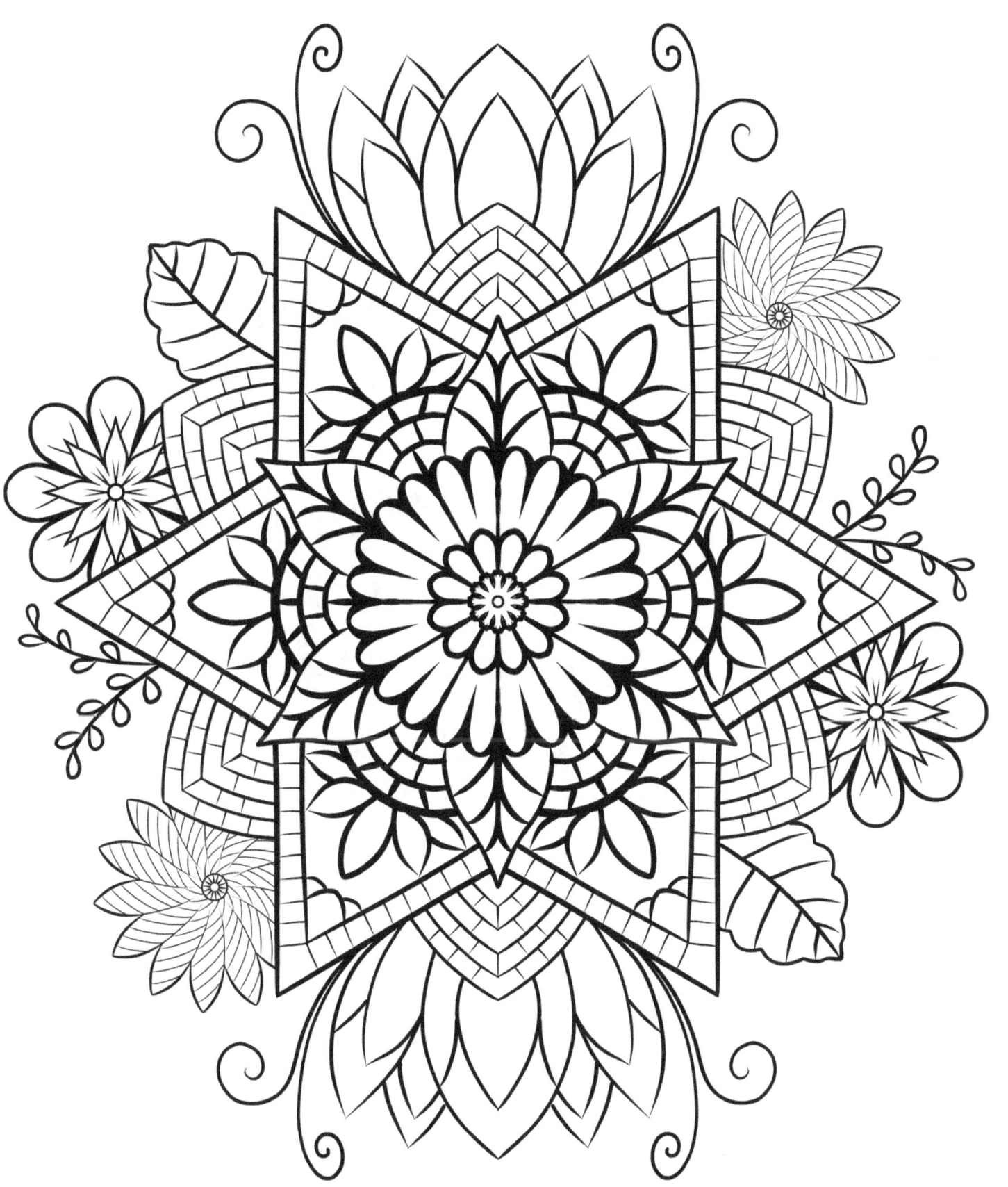

Bleed Through Barrier

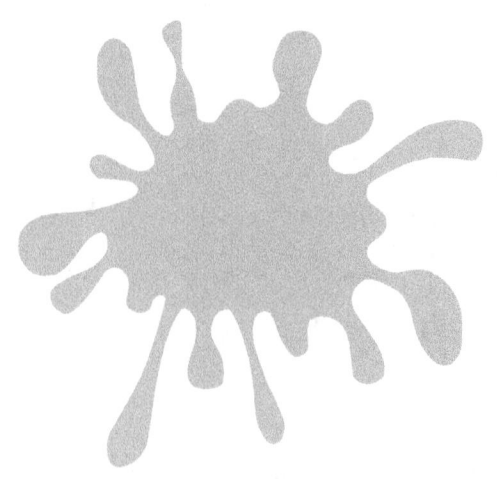

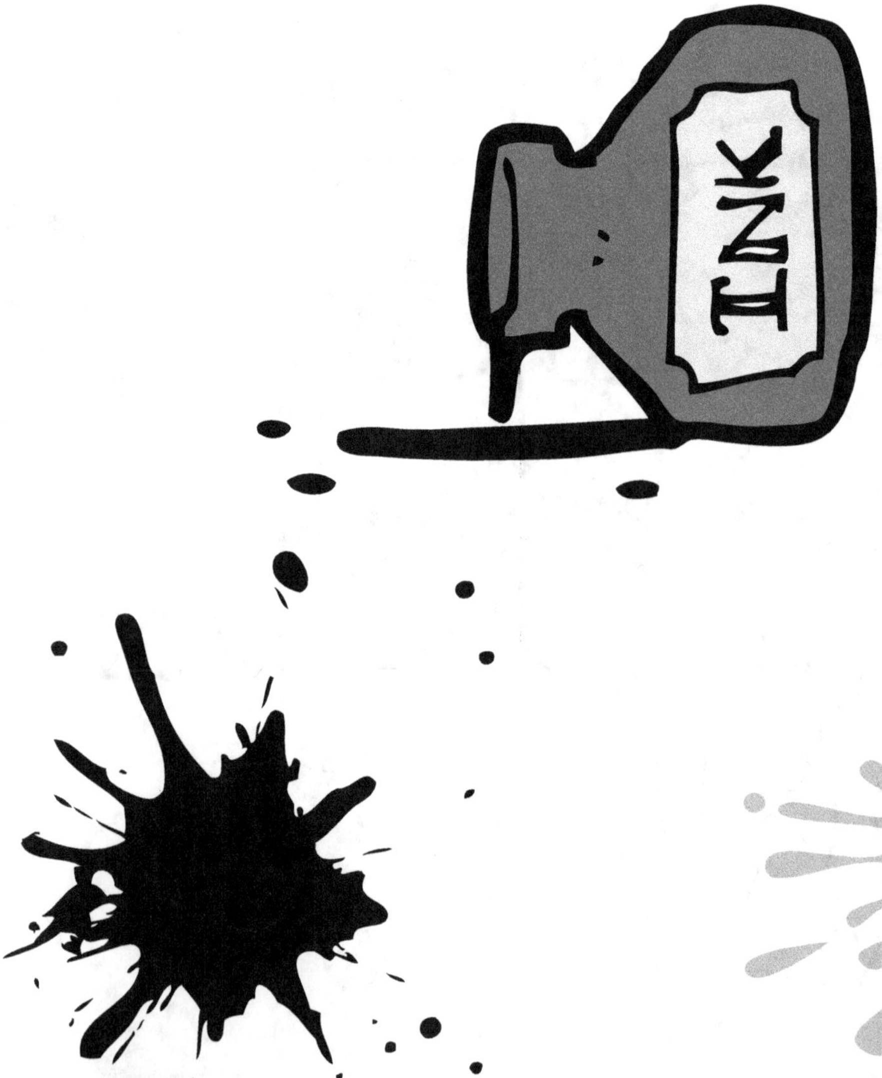

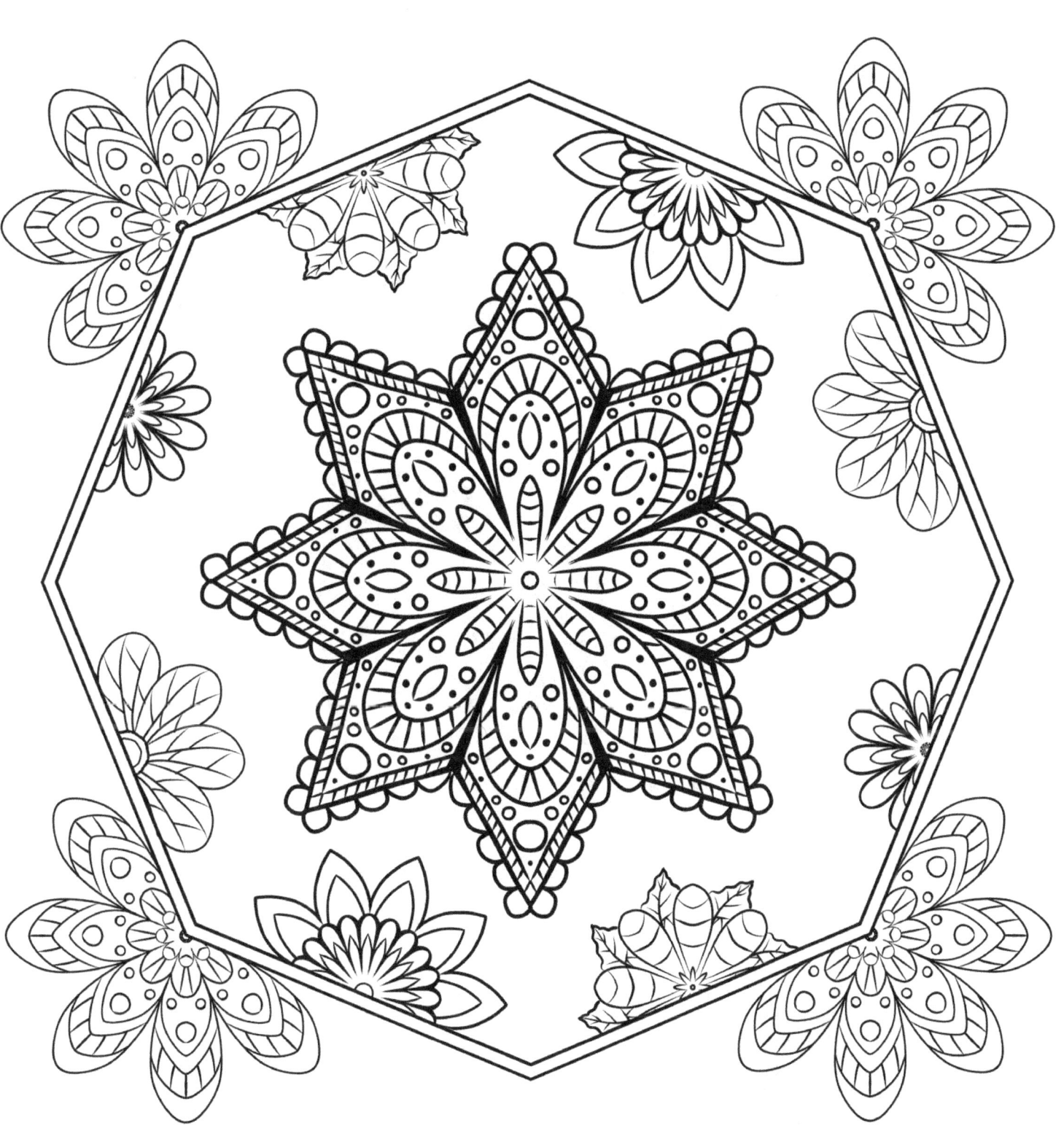

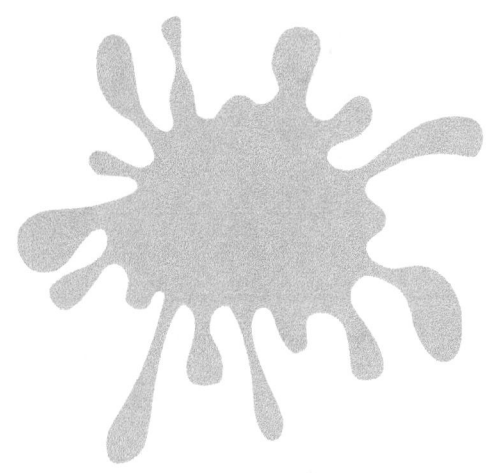

Bleed Through Barrier

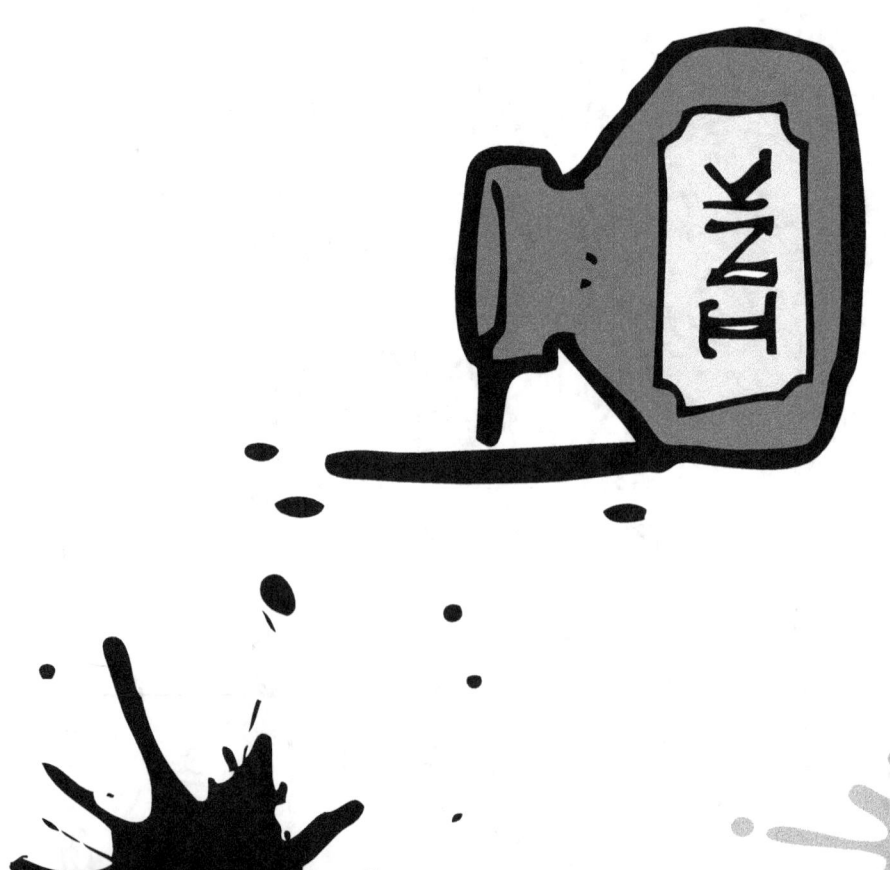

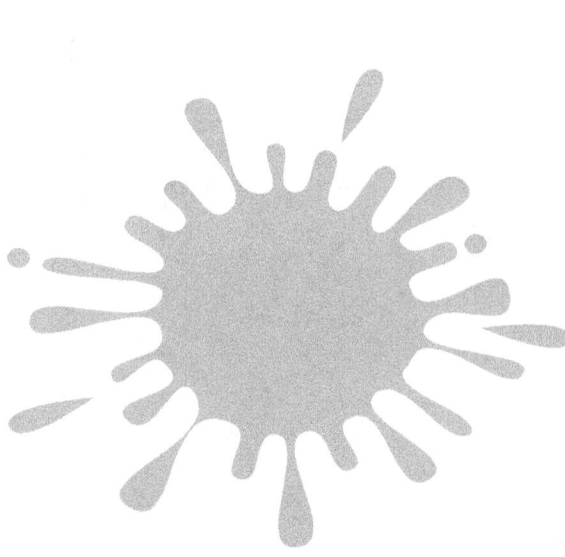

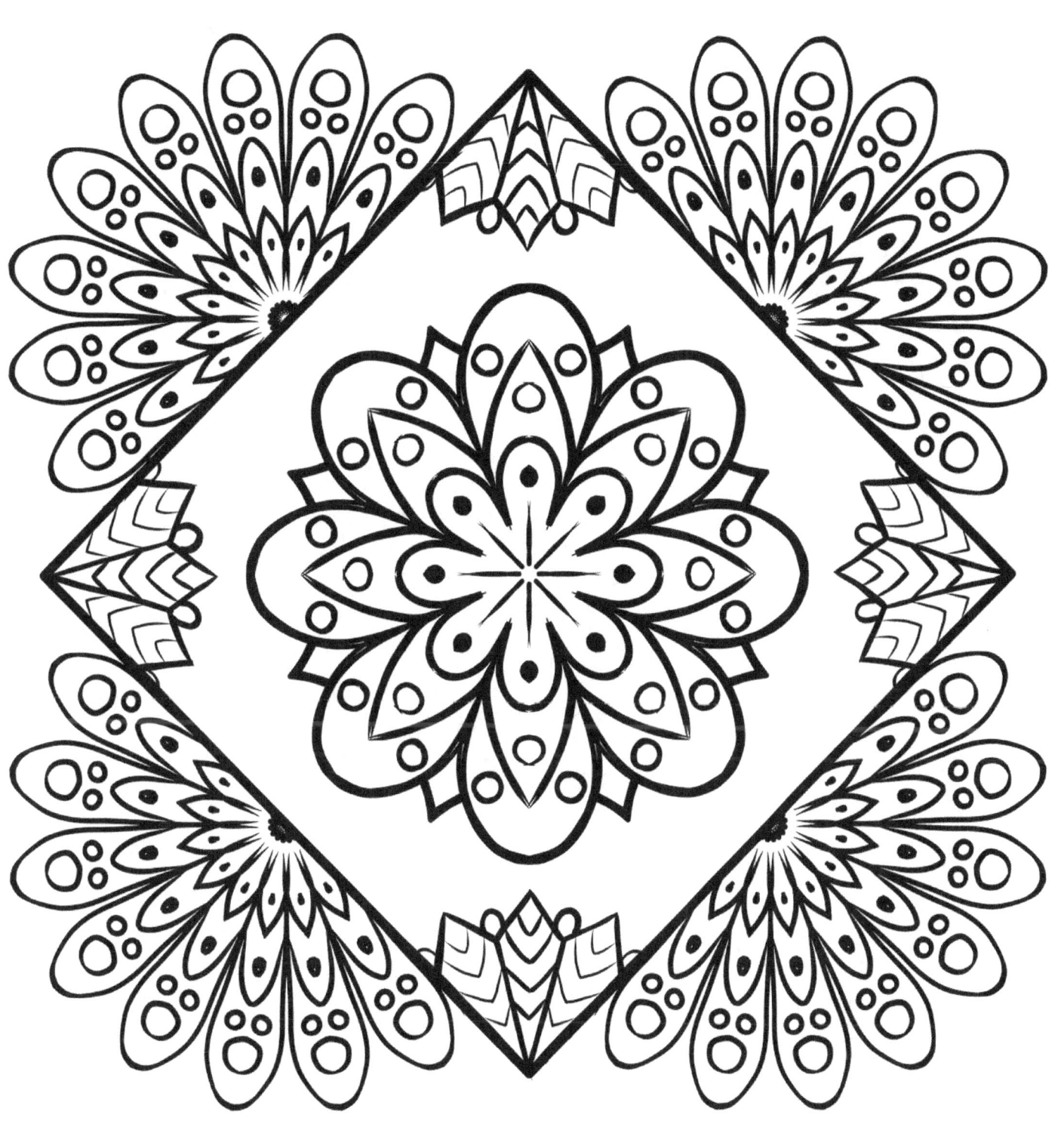

Bleed Through Barrier

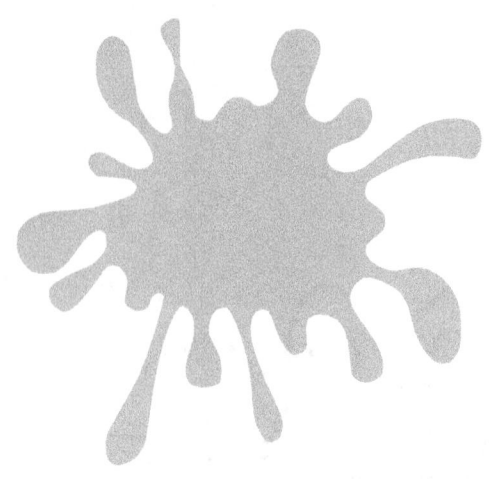

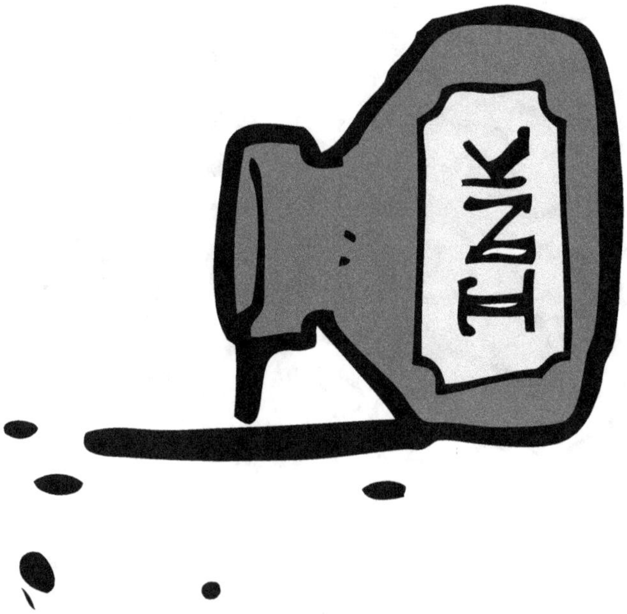

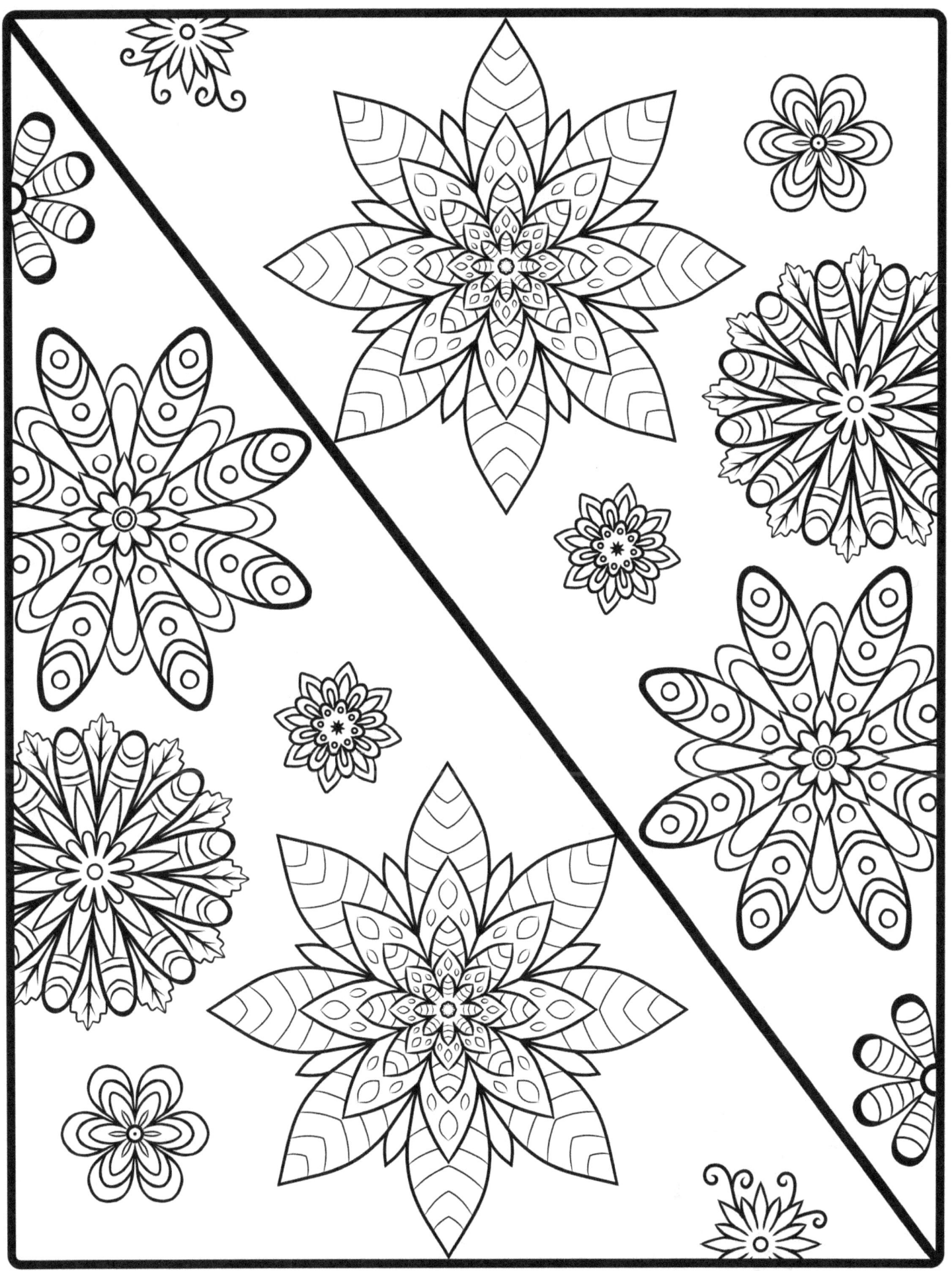

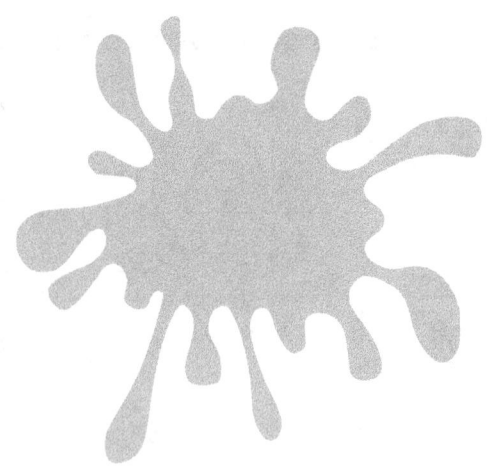

Bleed Through Barrier

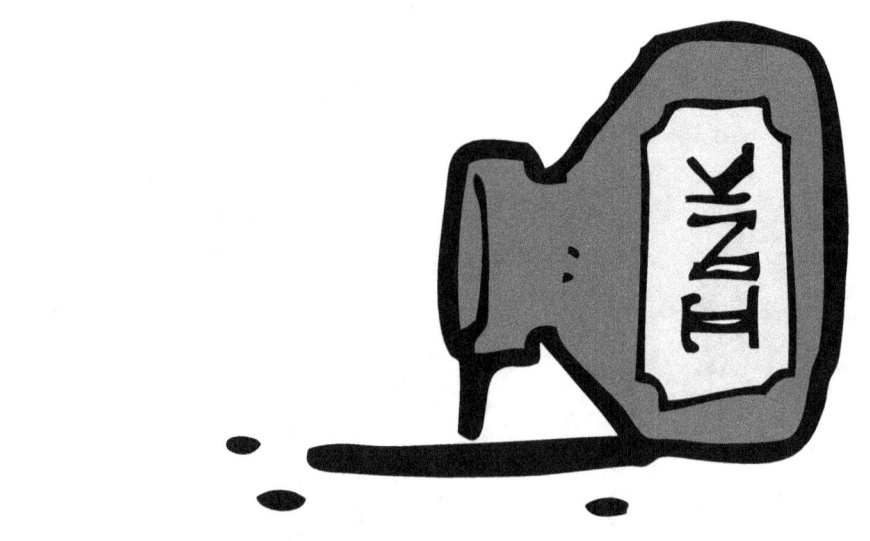

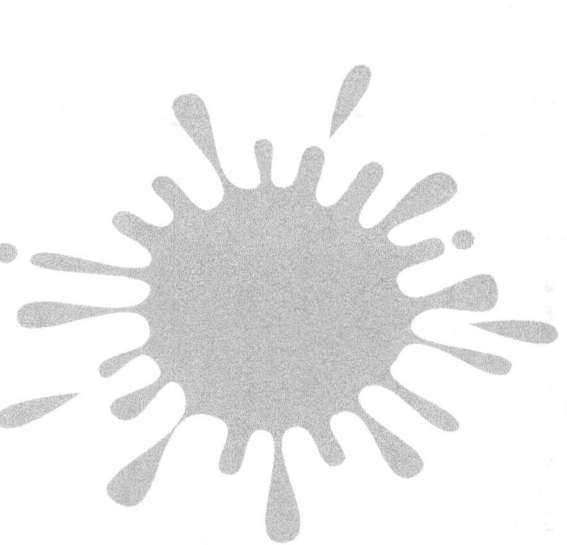

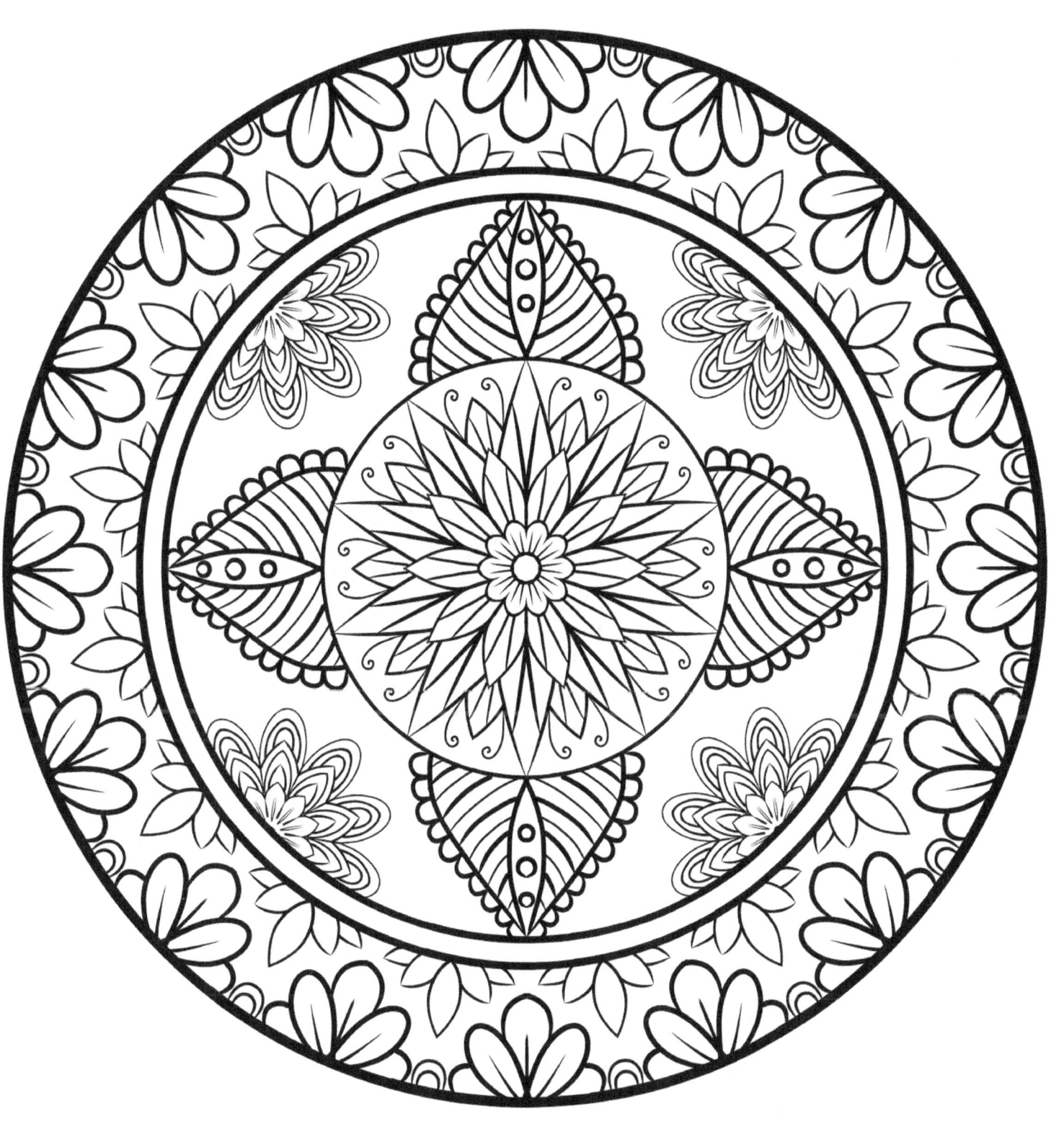

Bleed Through Barrier

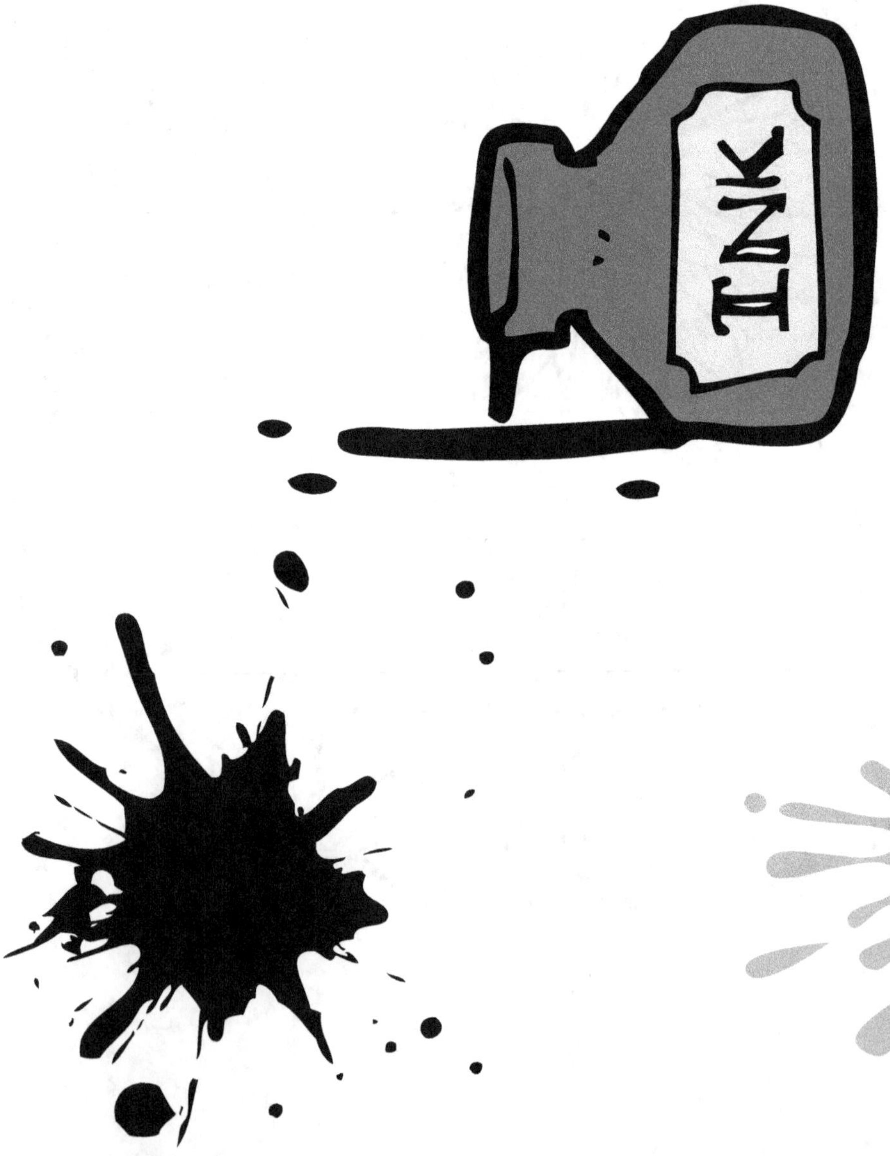

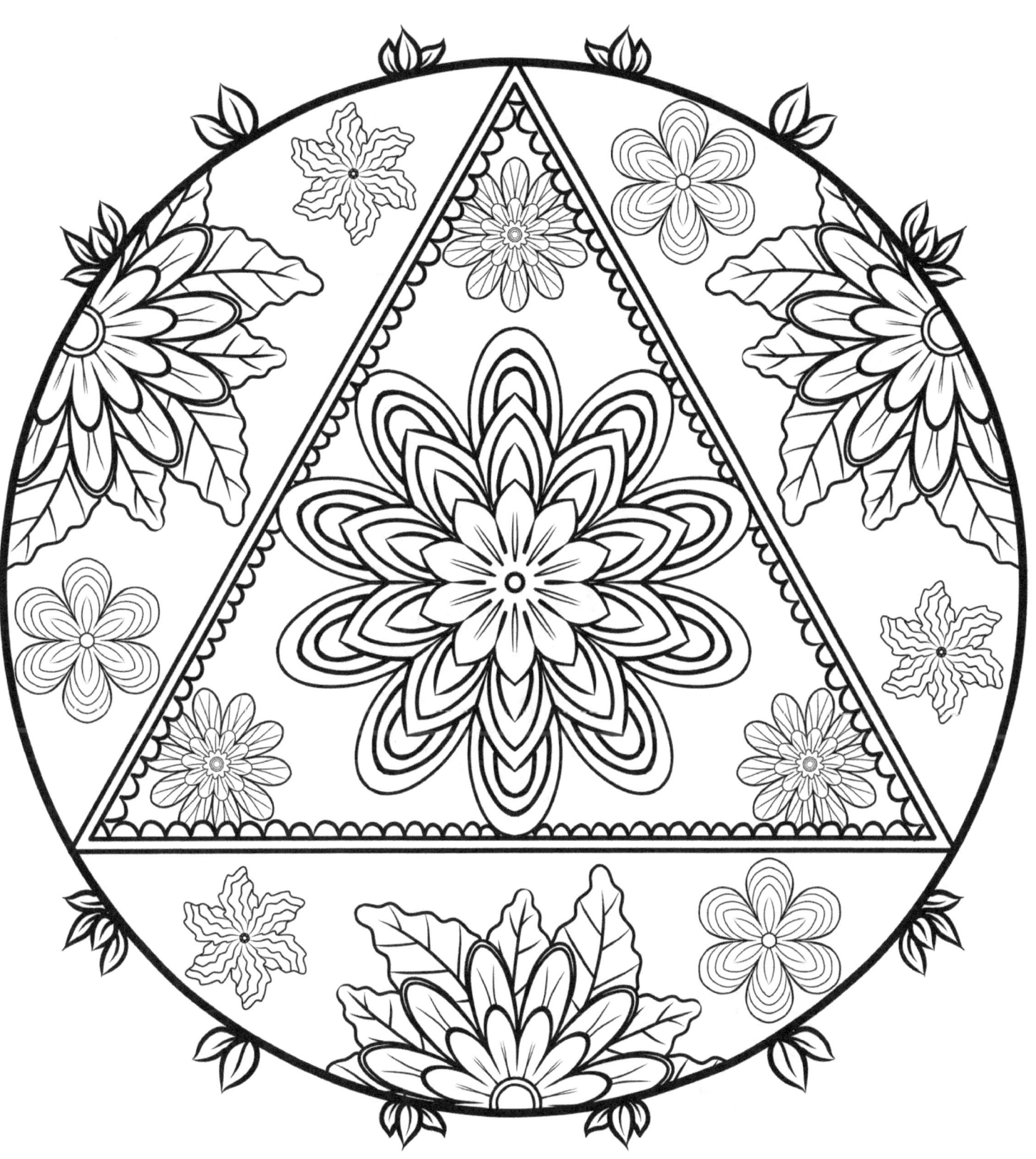

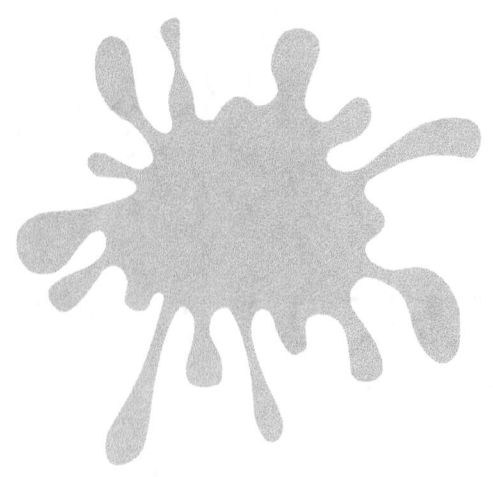

Bleed Through Barrier

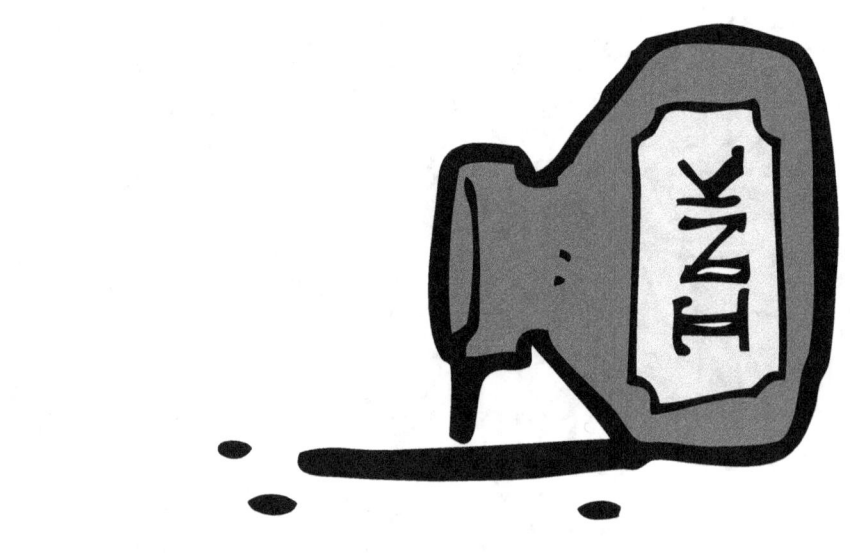

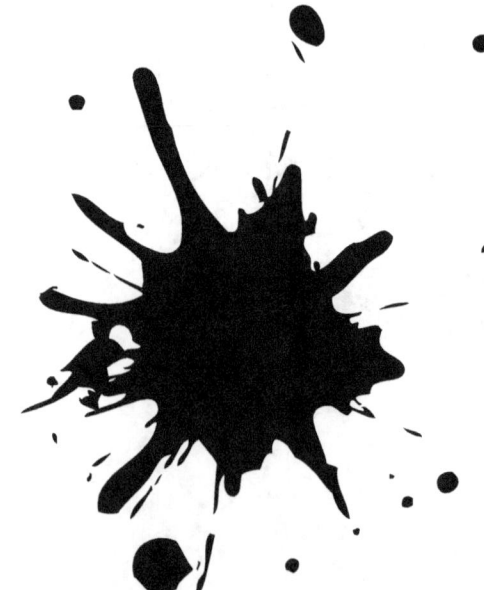

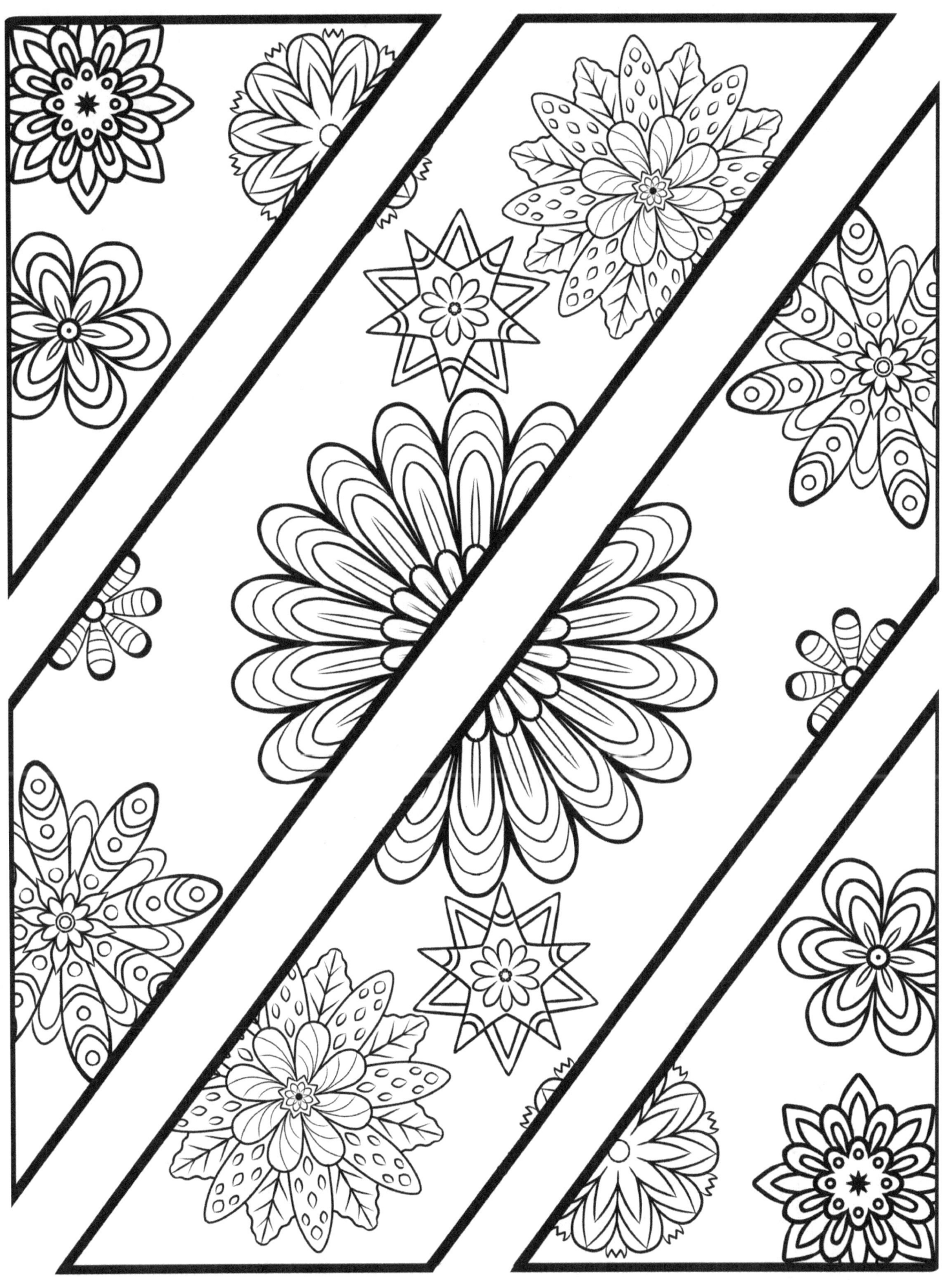

Bleed Through Barrier

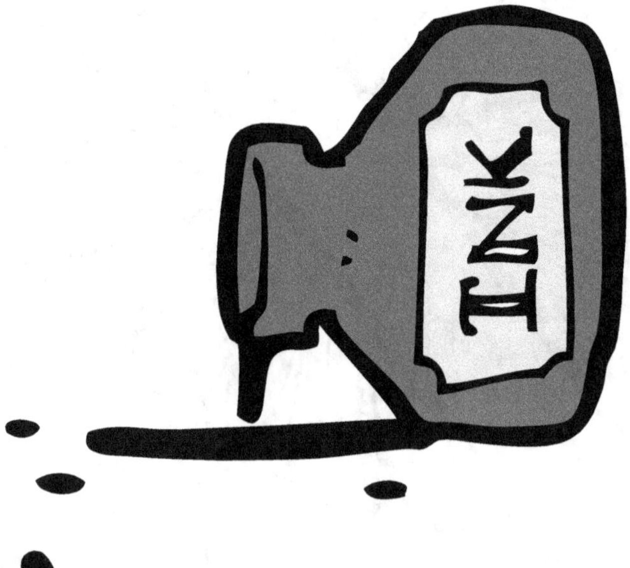

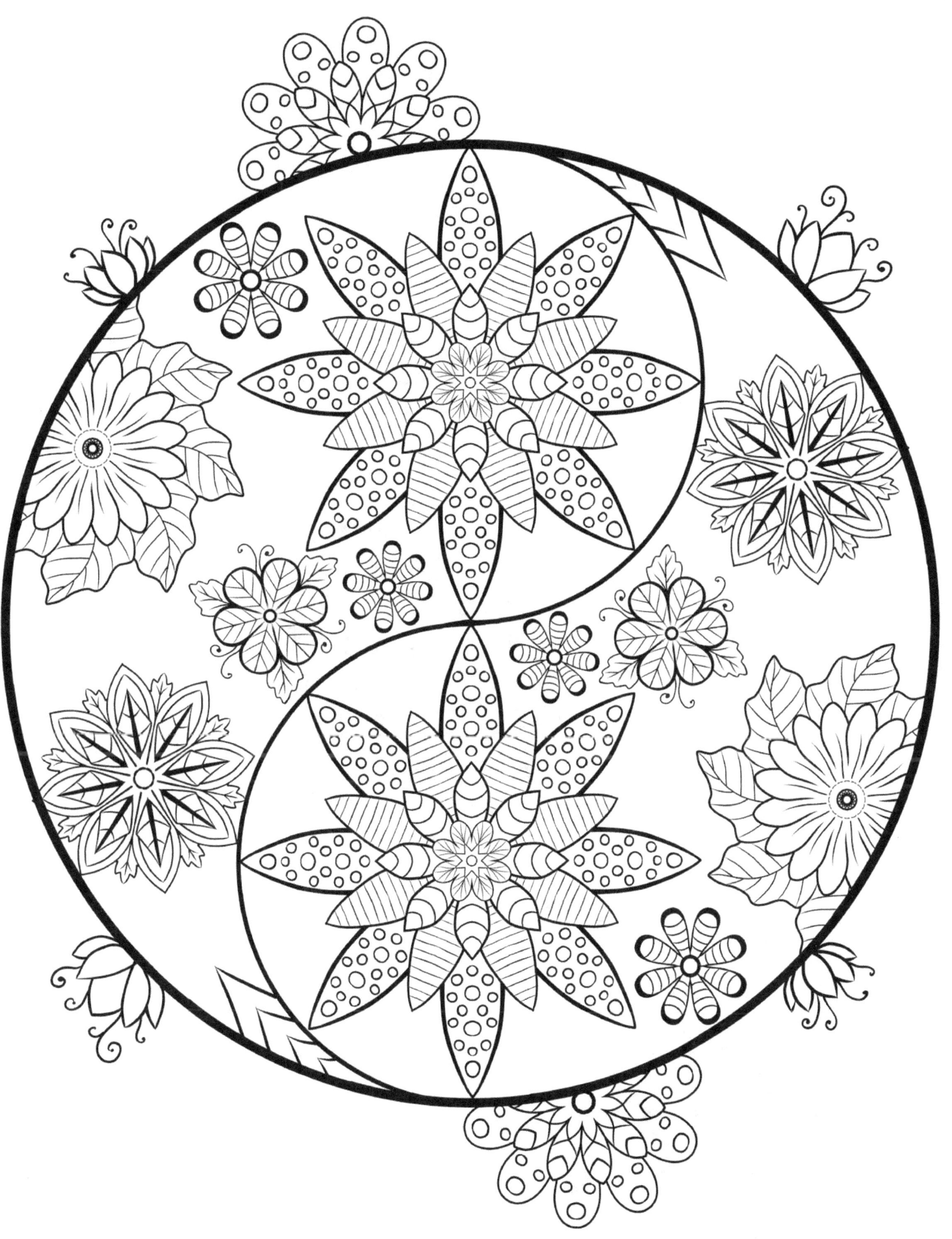

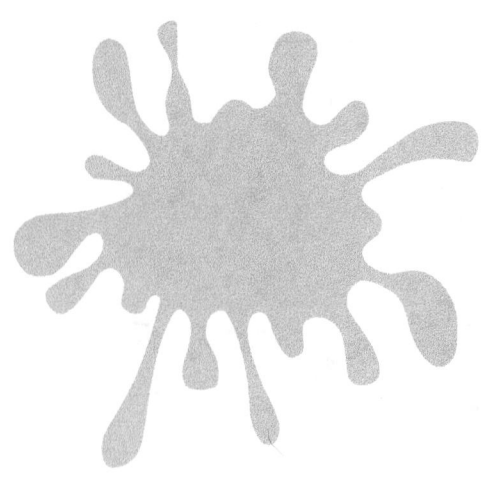

Bleed Through Barrier

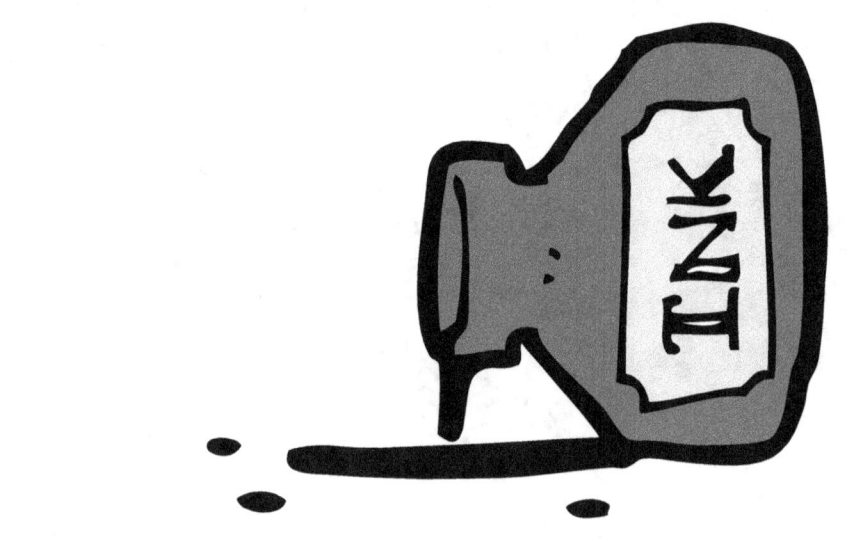

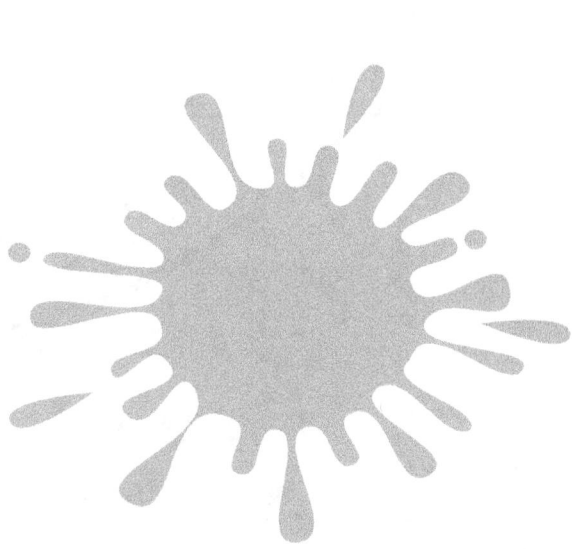

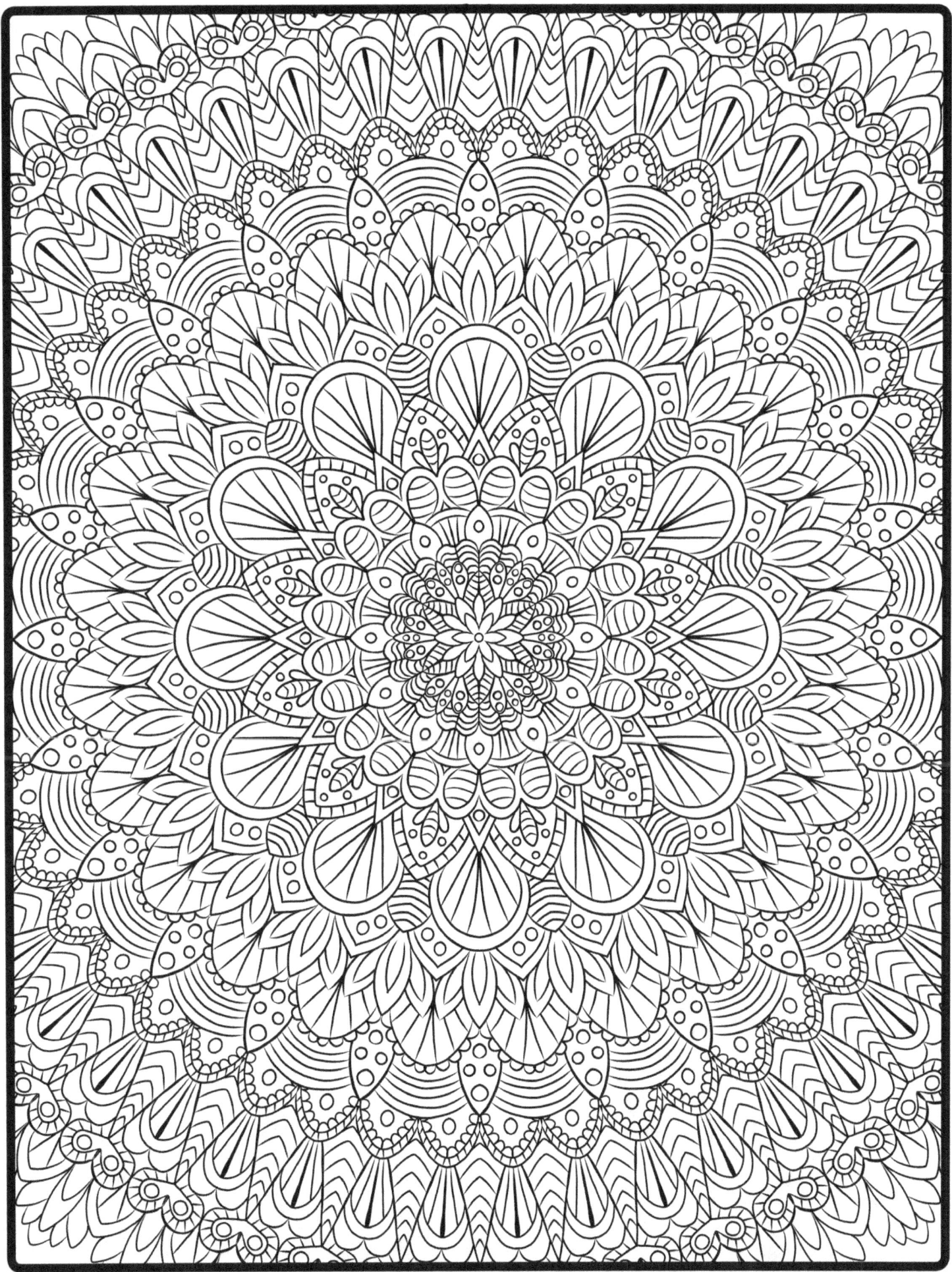

Bleed Through Barrier

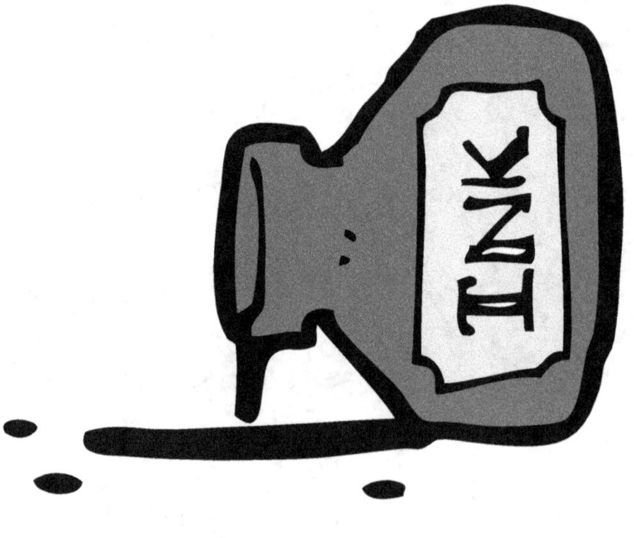

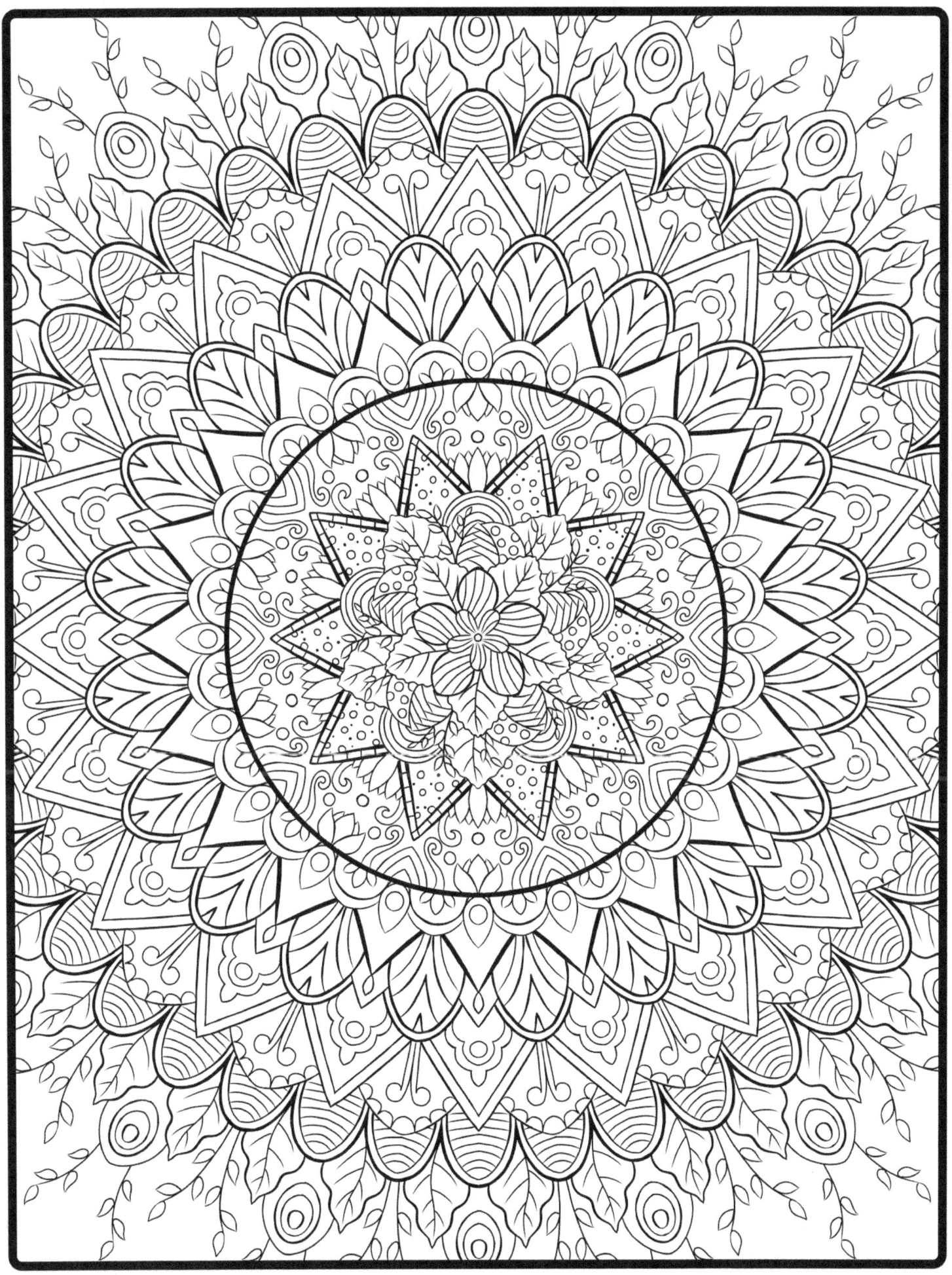

Bleed Through Barrier

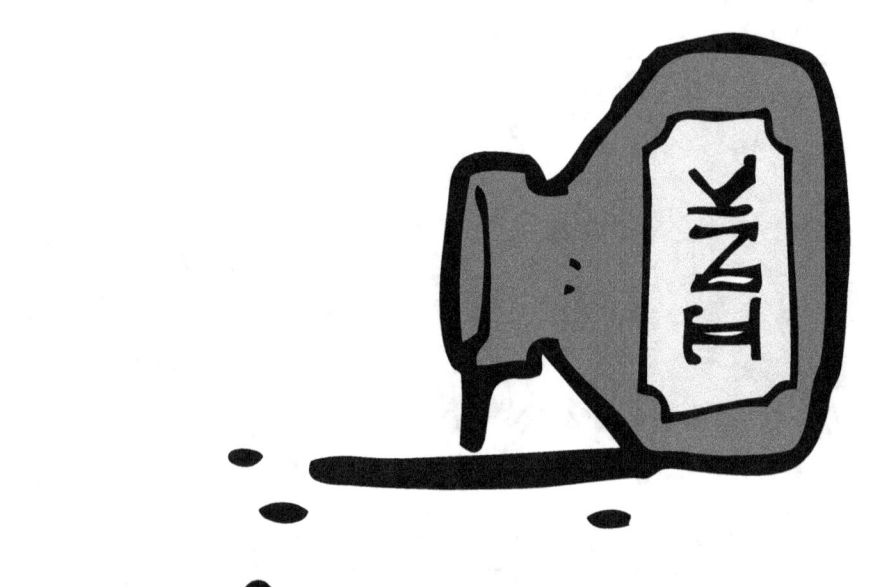

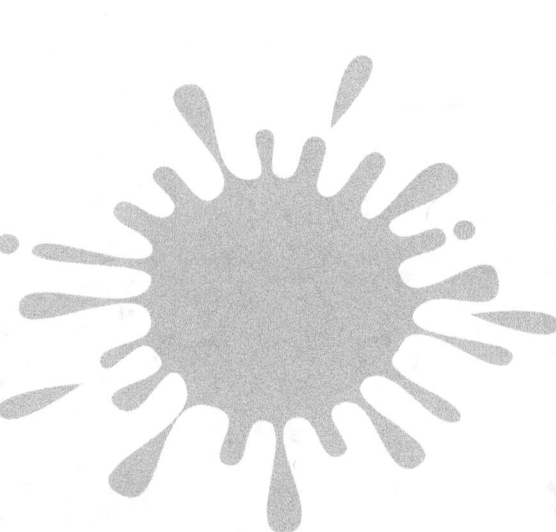

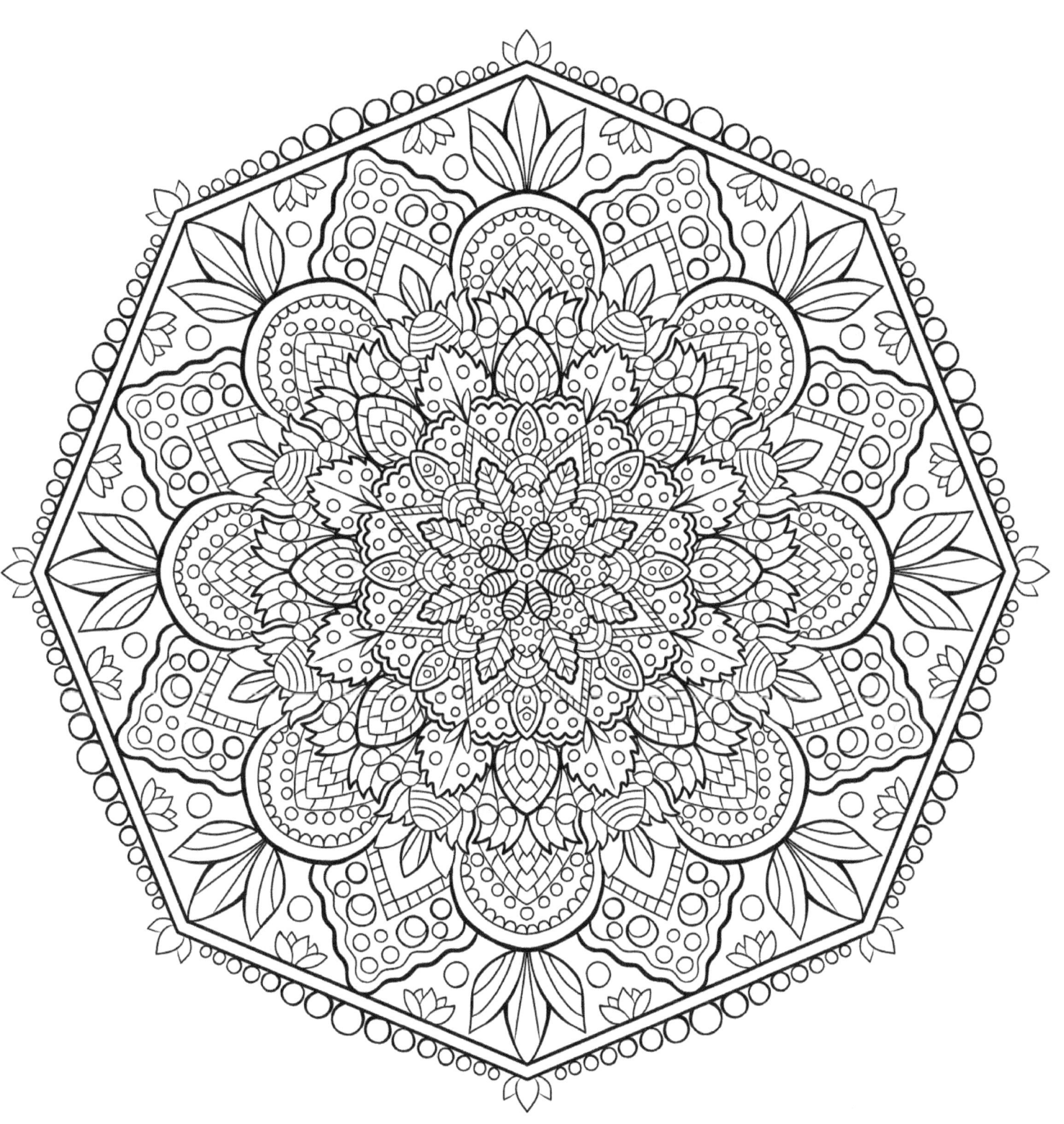

Bleed Through Barrier

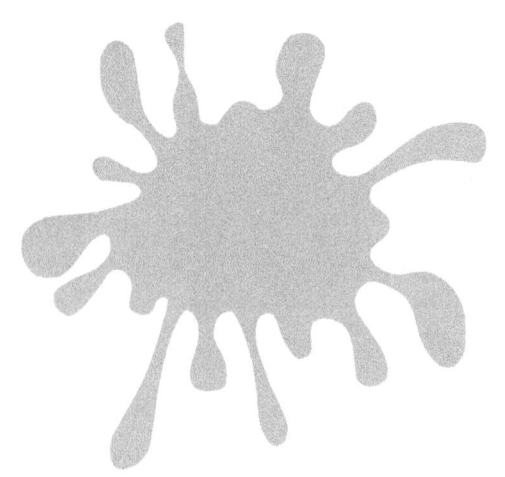

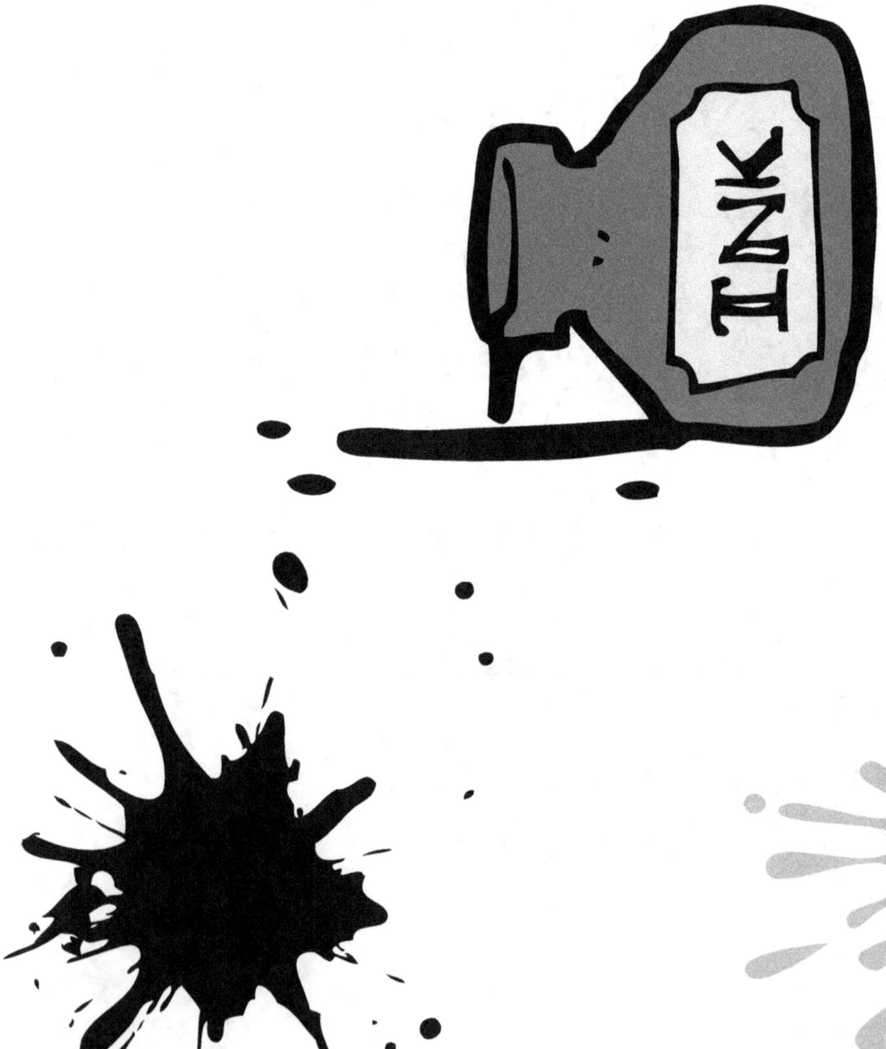

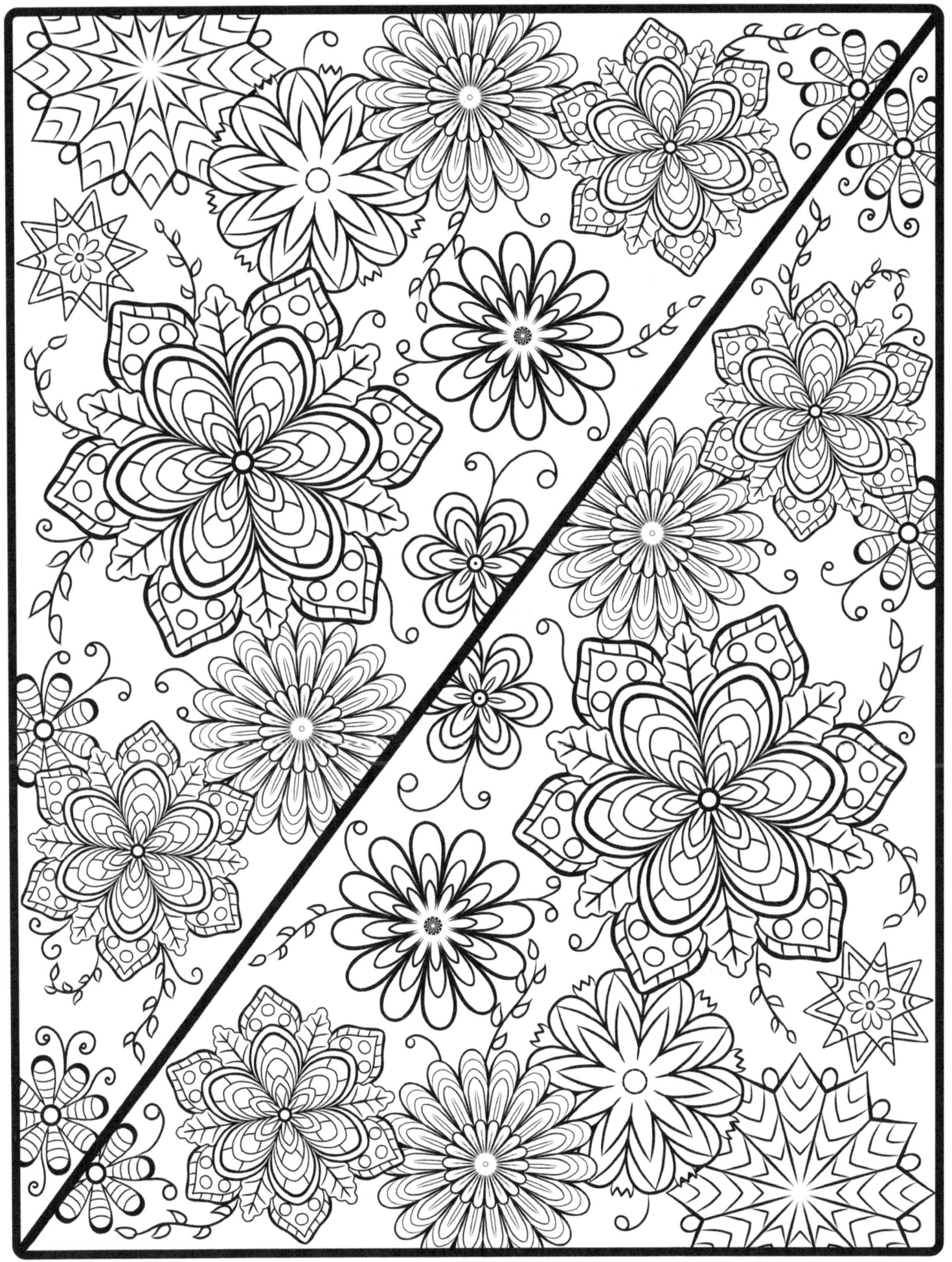

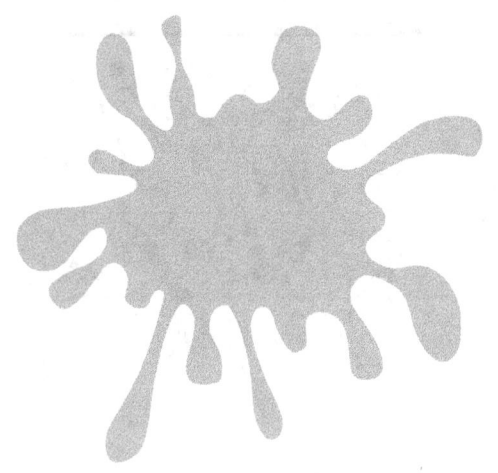

Bleed Through Barrier

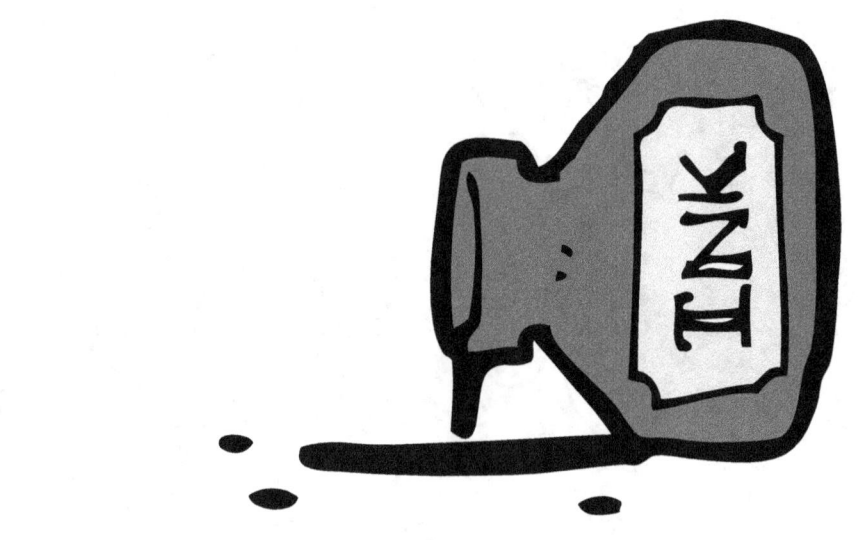

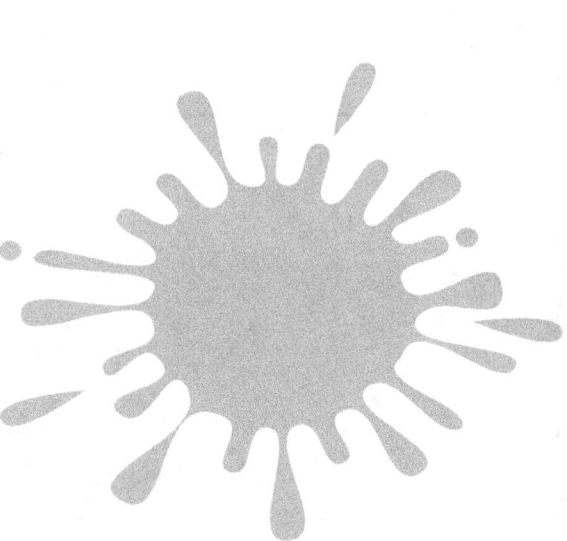

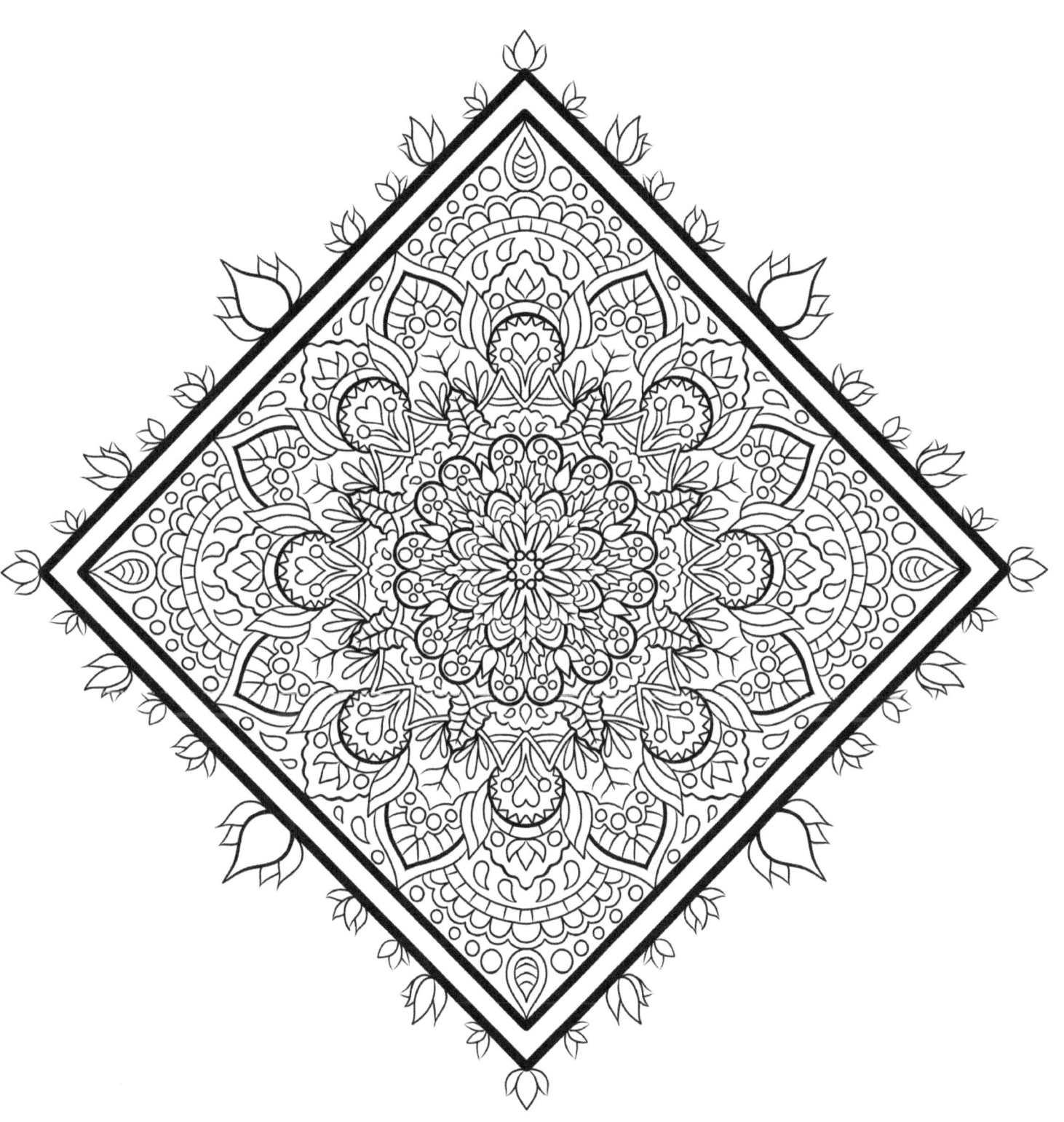

Bleed Through Barrier

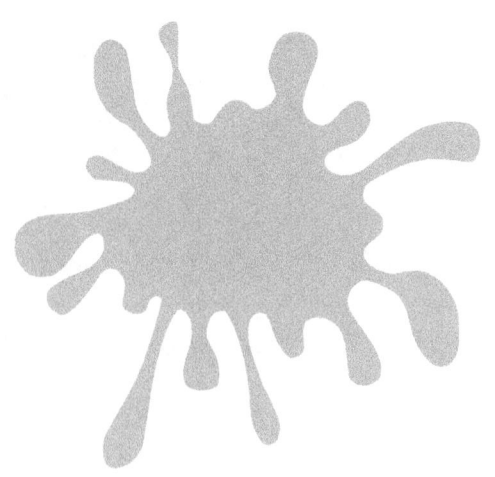

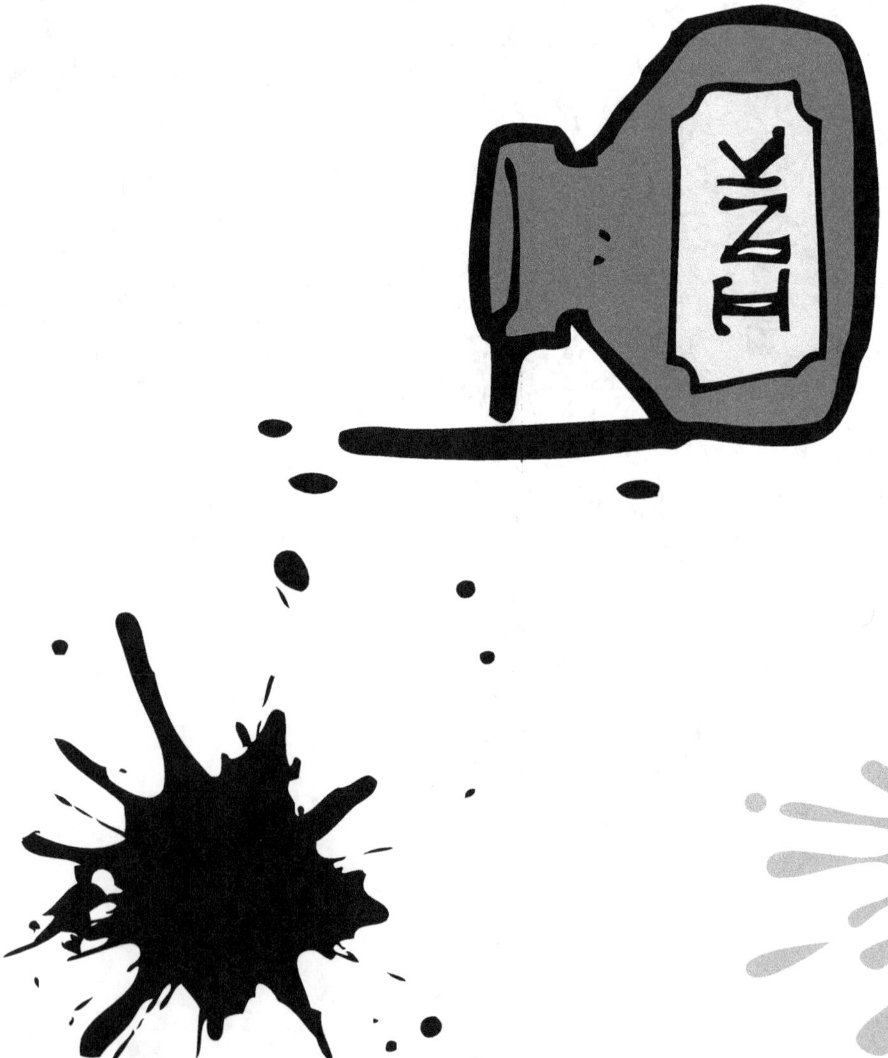

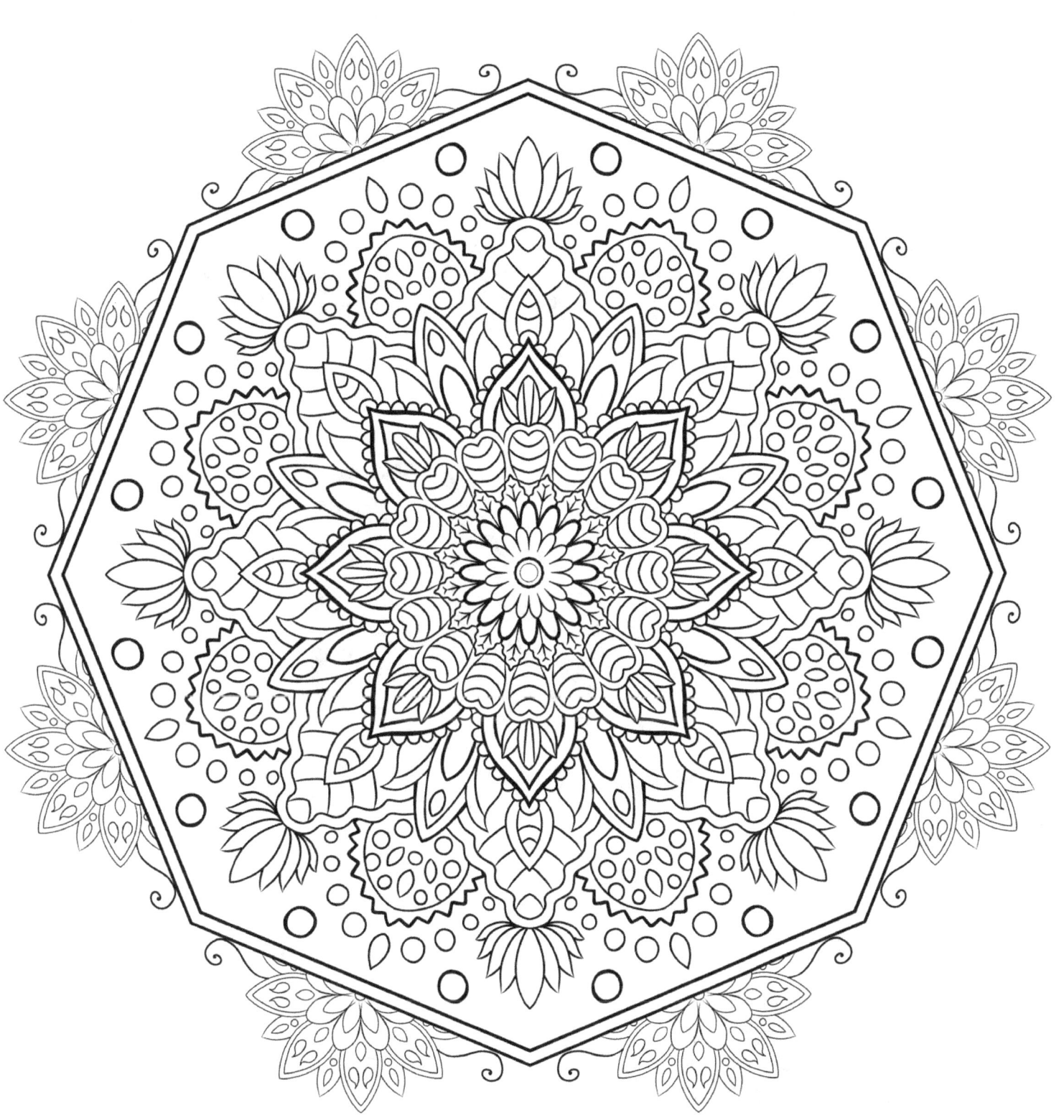

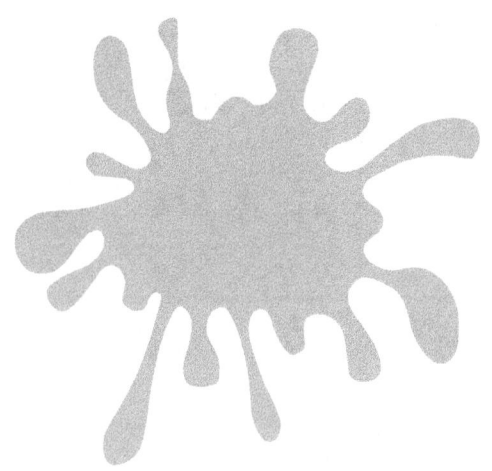

Bleed Through Barrier

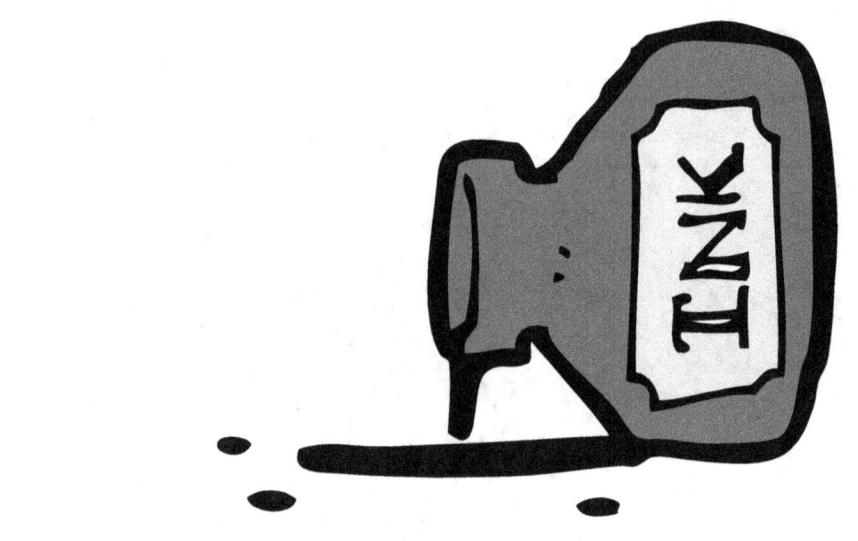

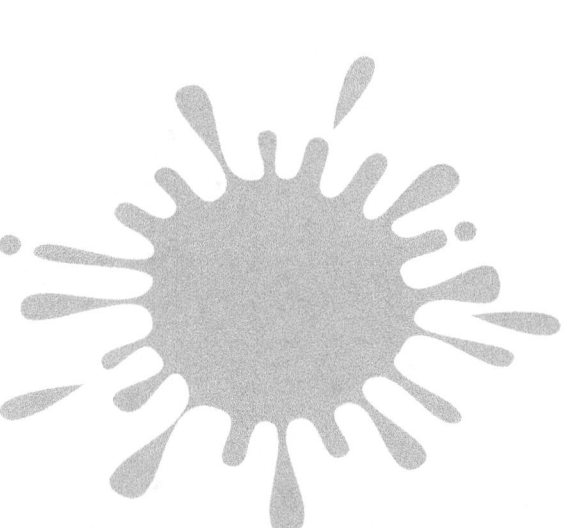

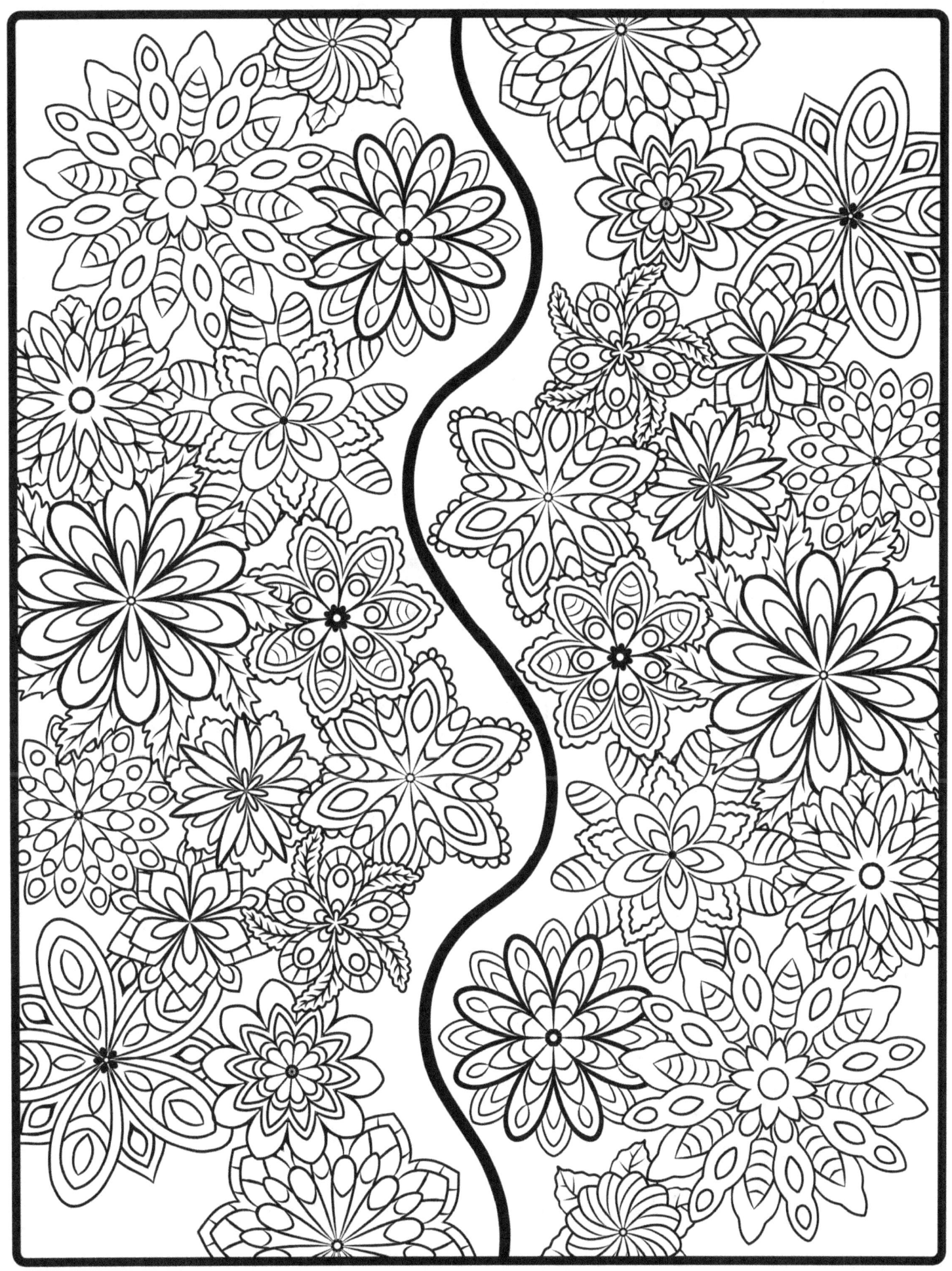

Bleed Through Barrier

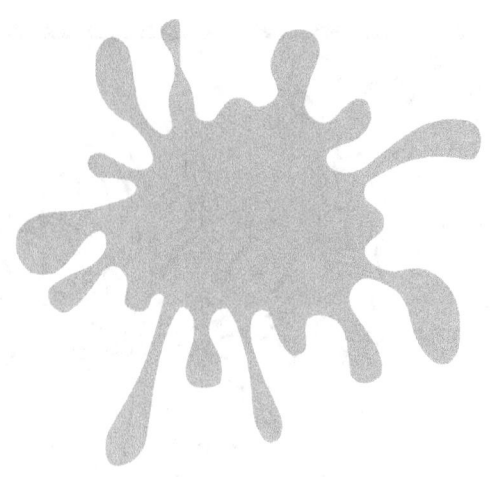

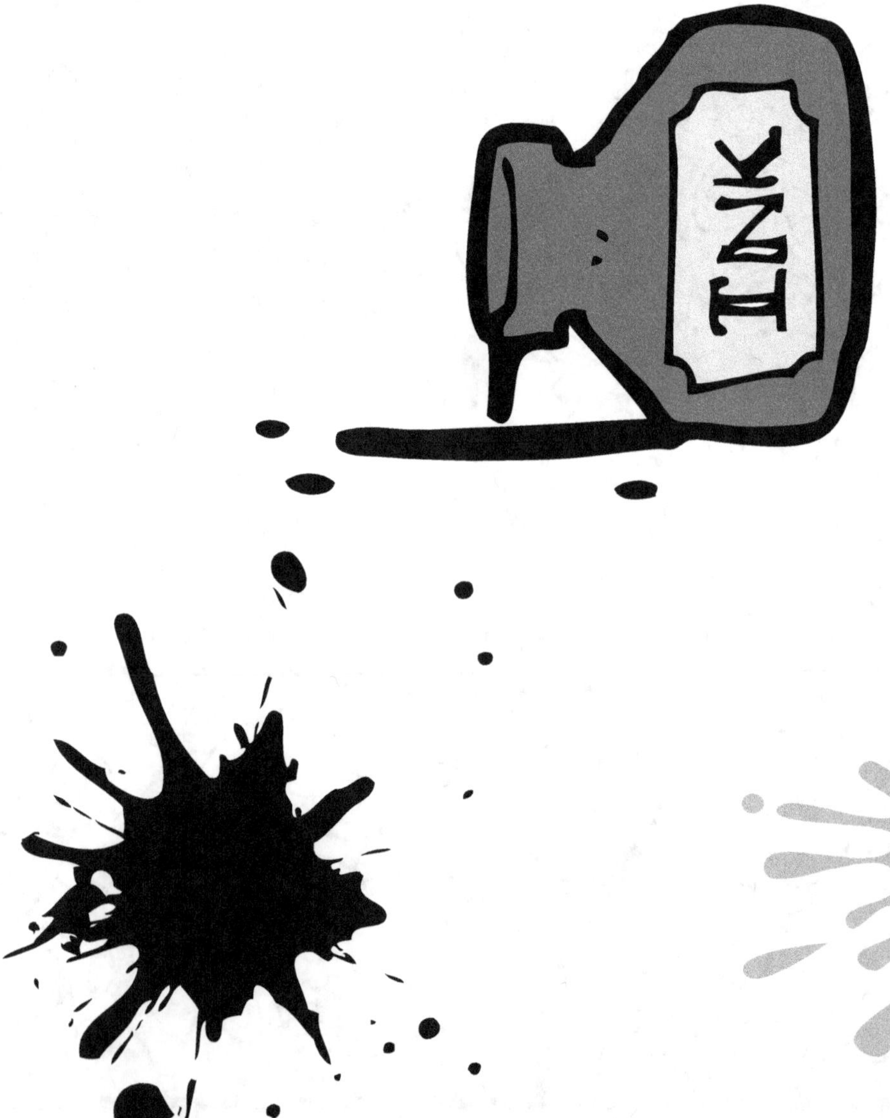

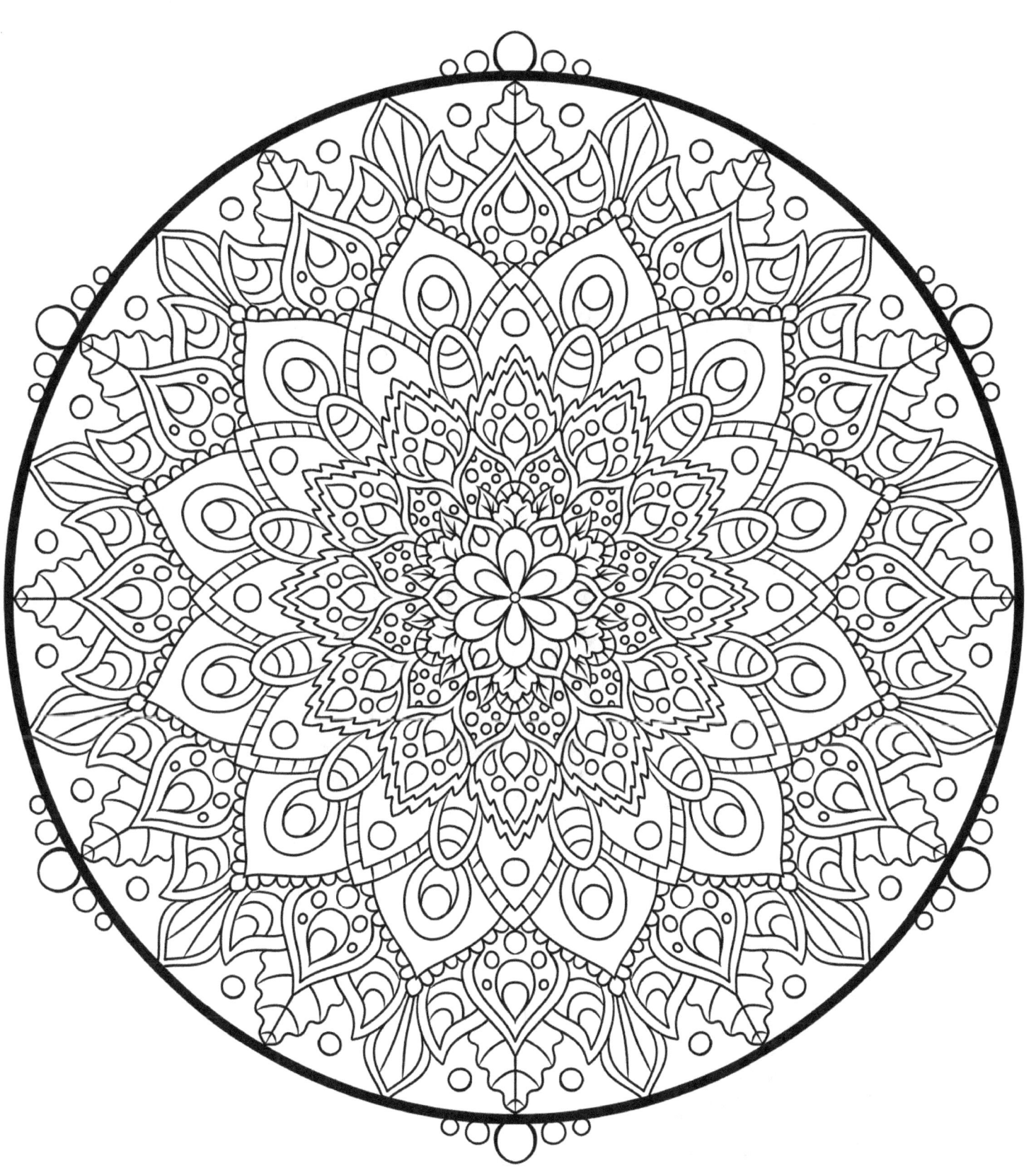

Bleed Through Barrier

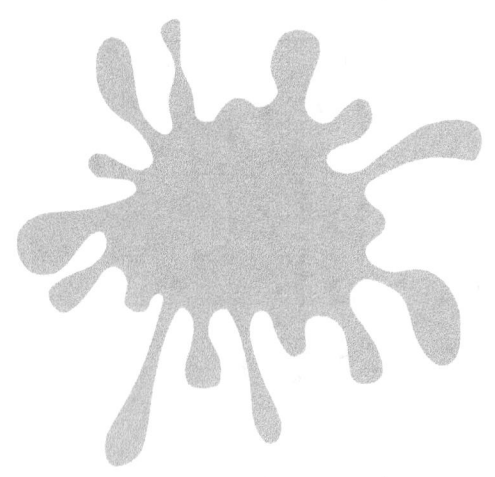

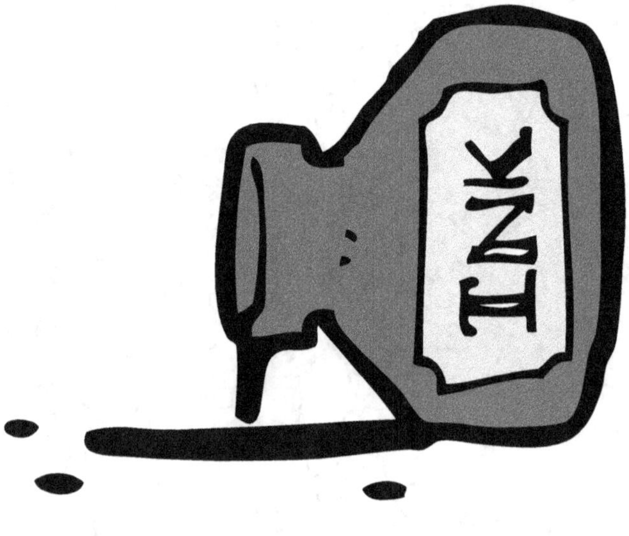

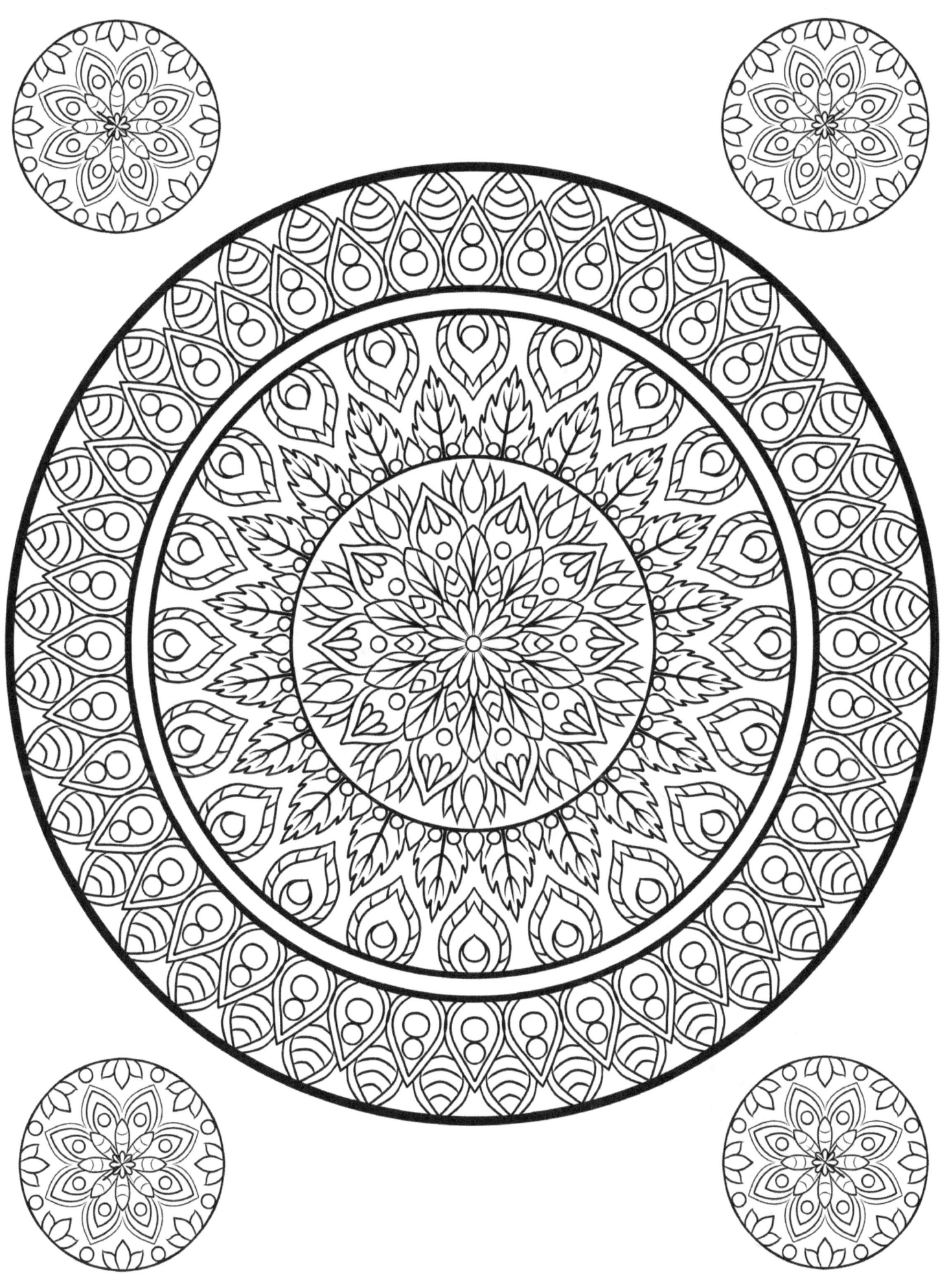

Bleed Through Barrier

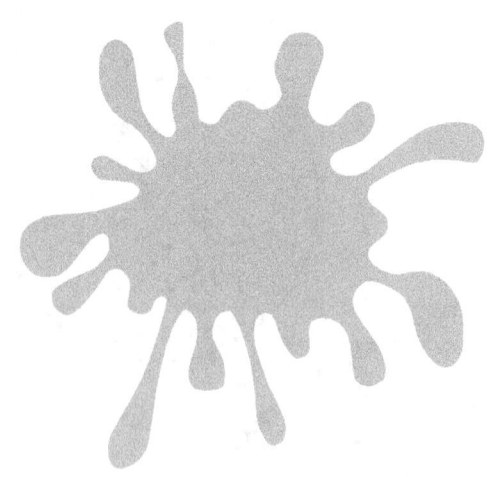

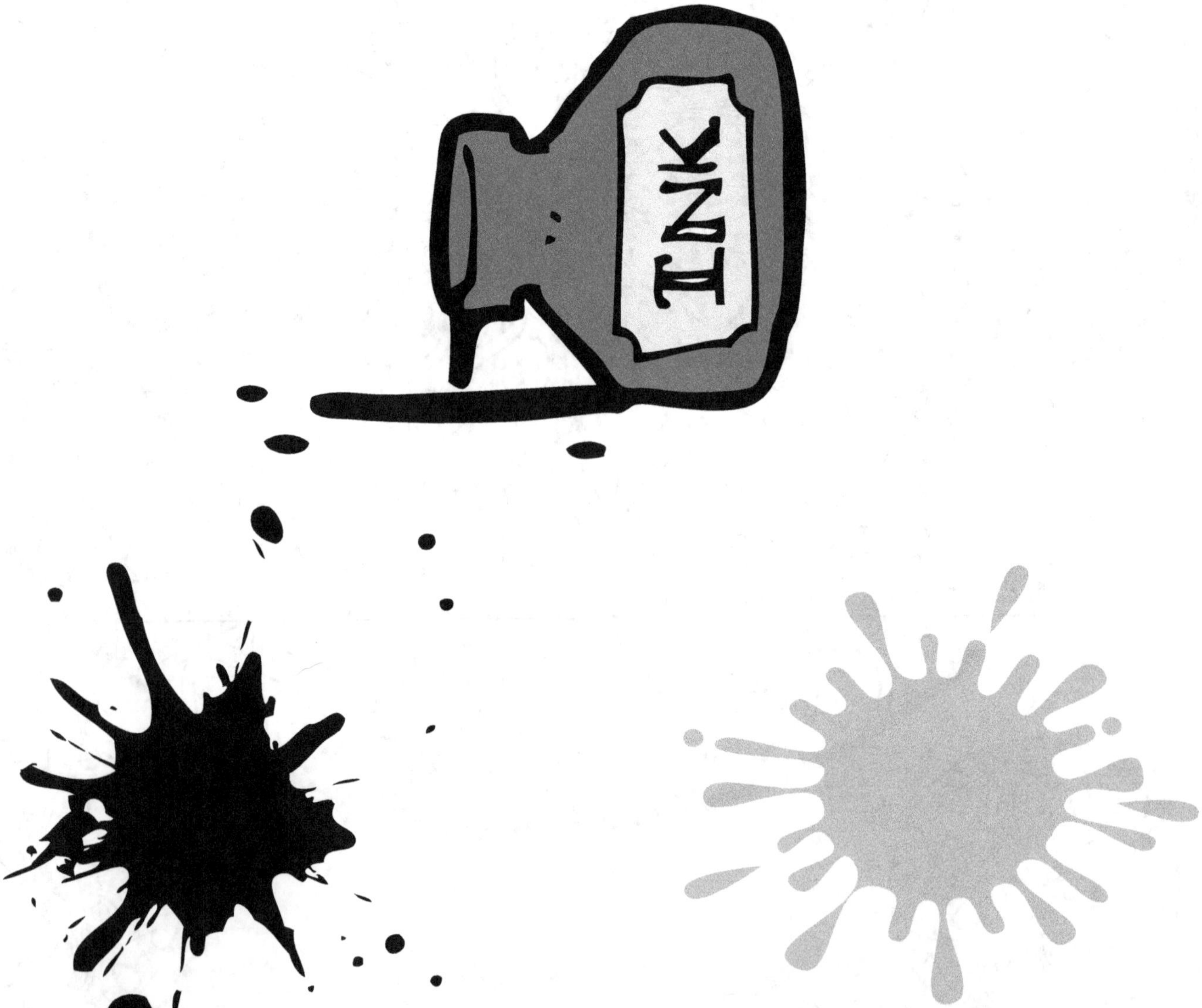

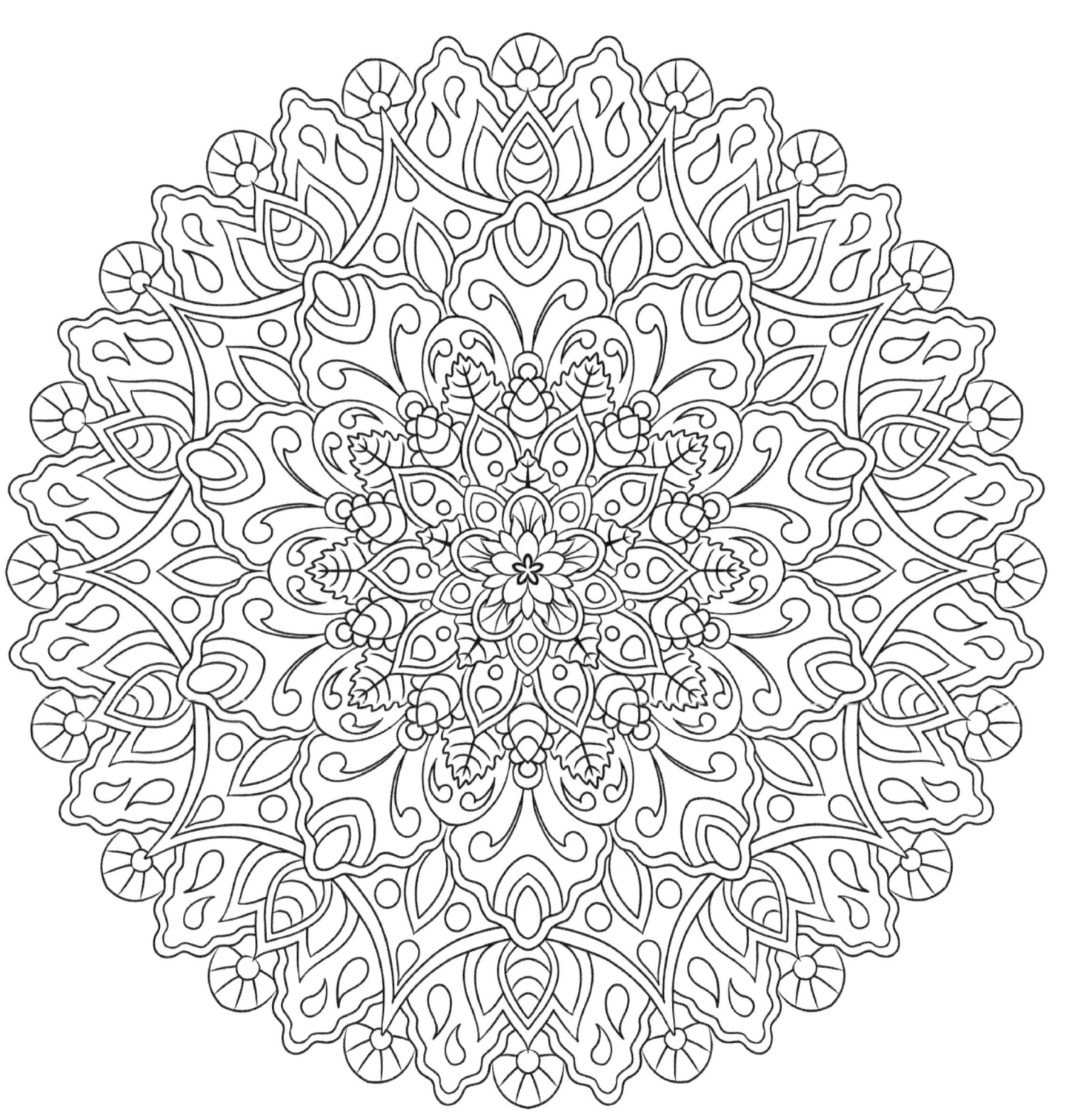

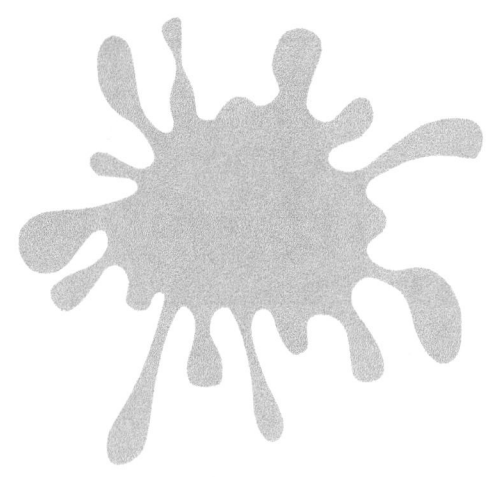

Bleed Through Barrier

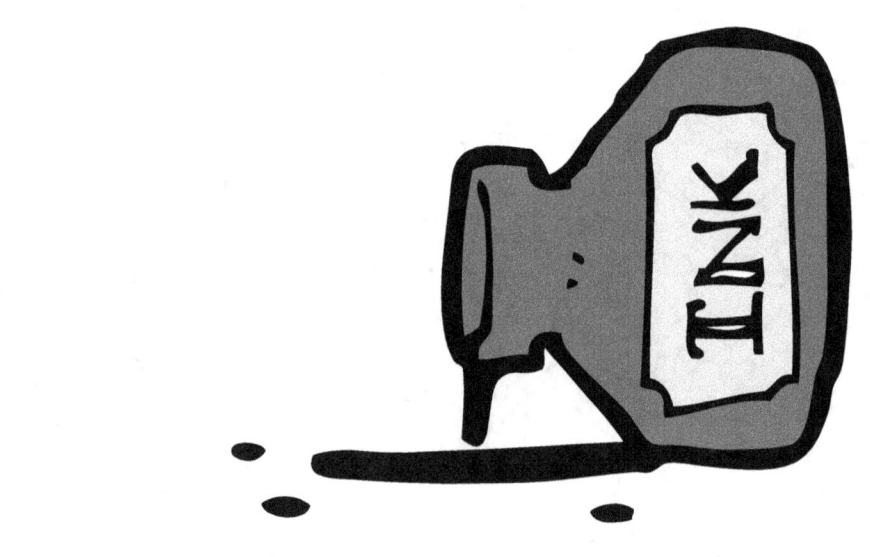

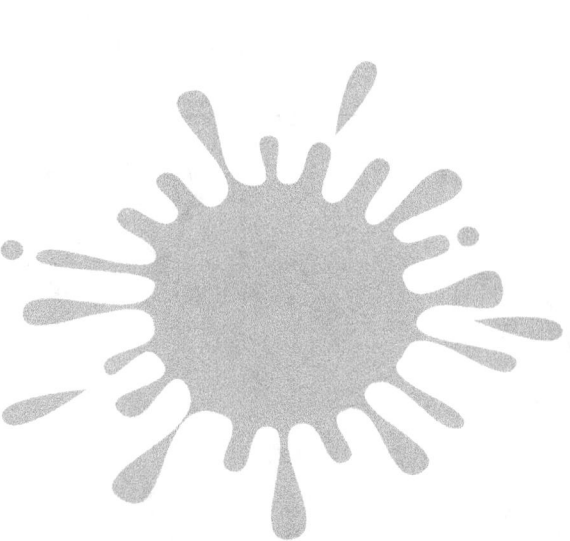

Bleed Through Barrier

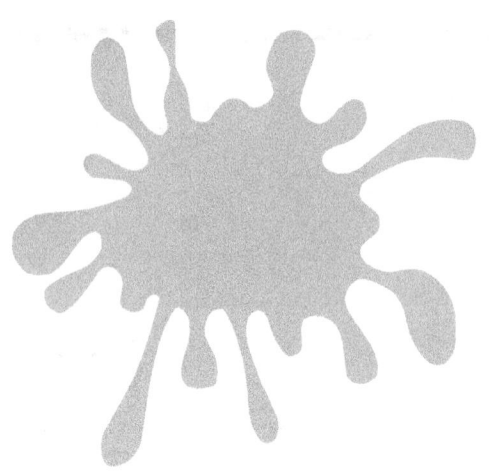

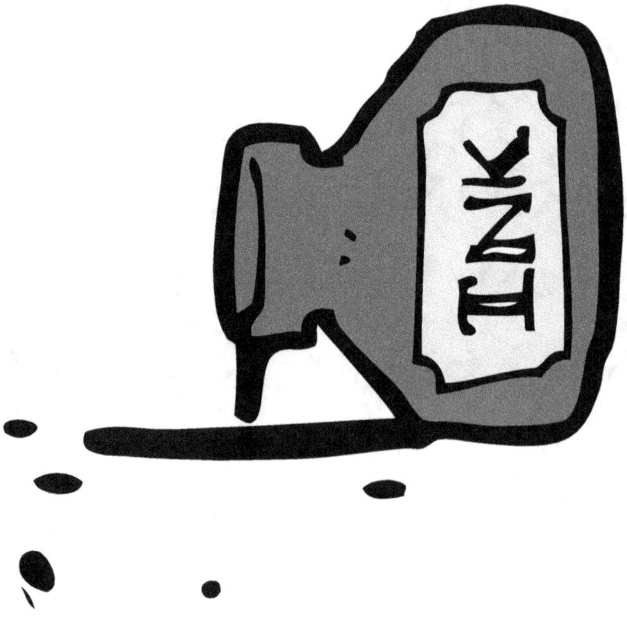

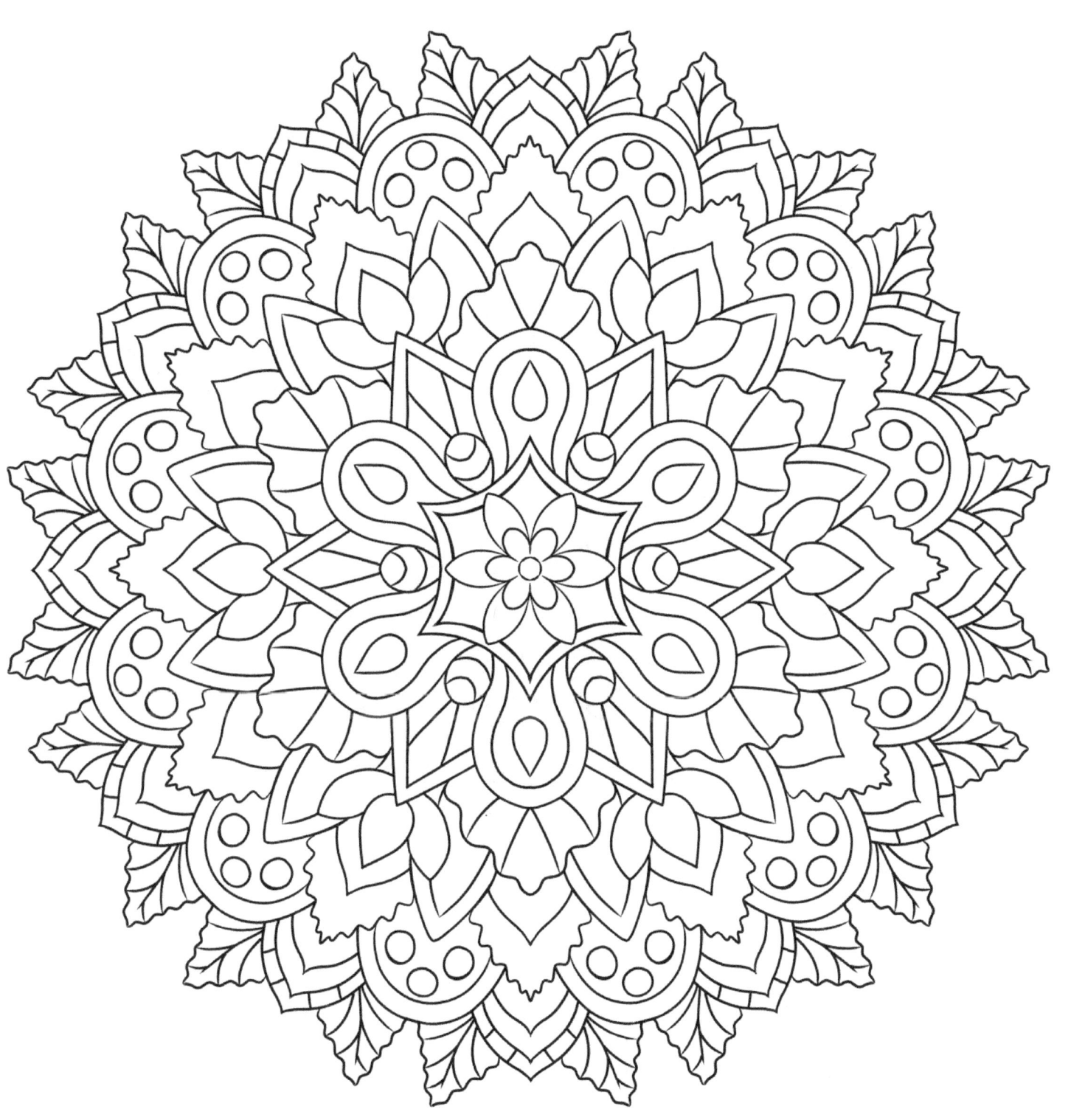

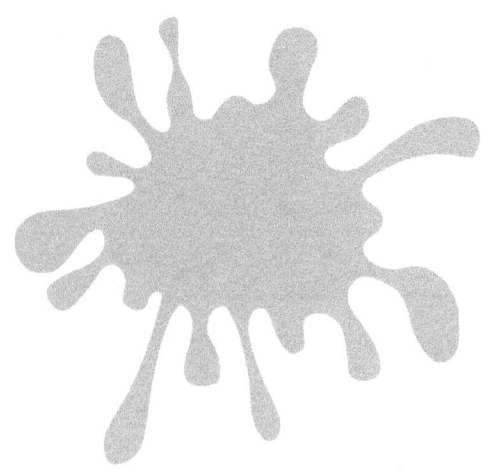

Bleed Through Barrier

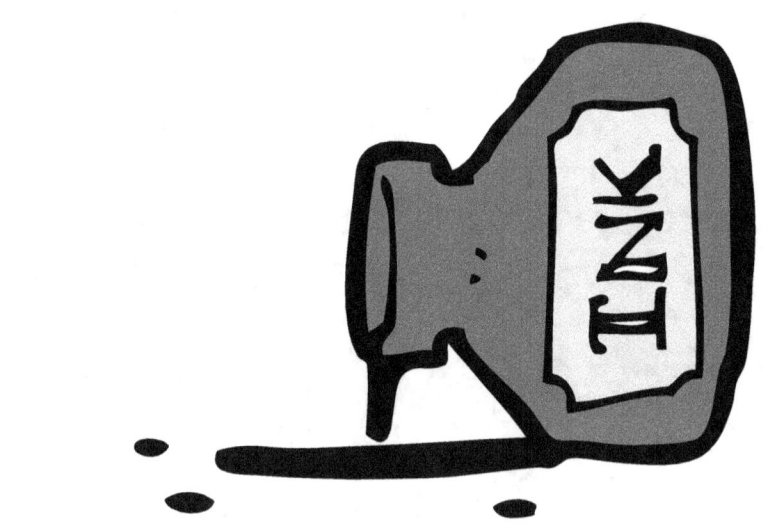

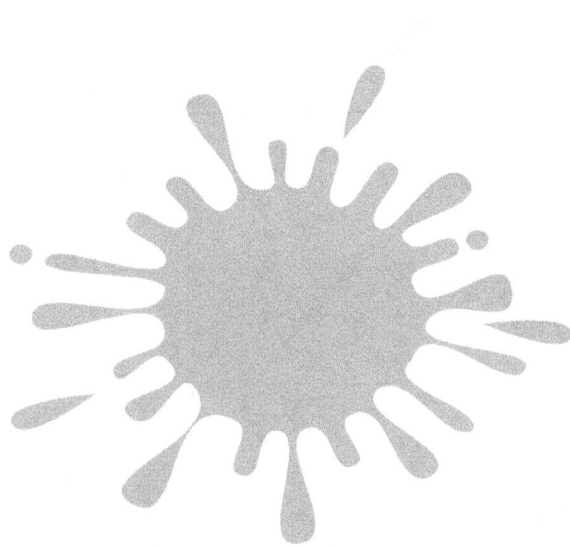

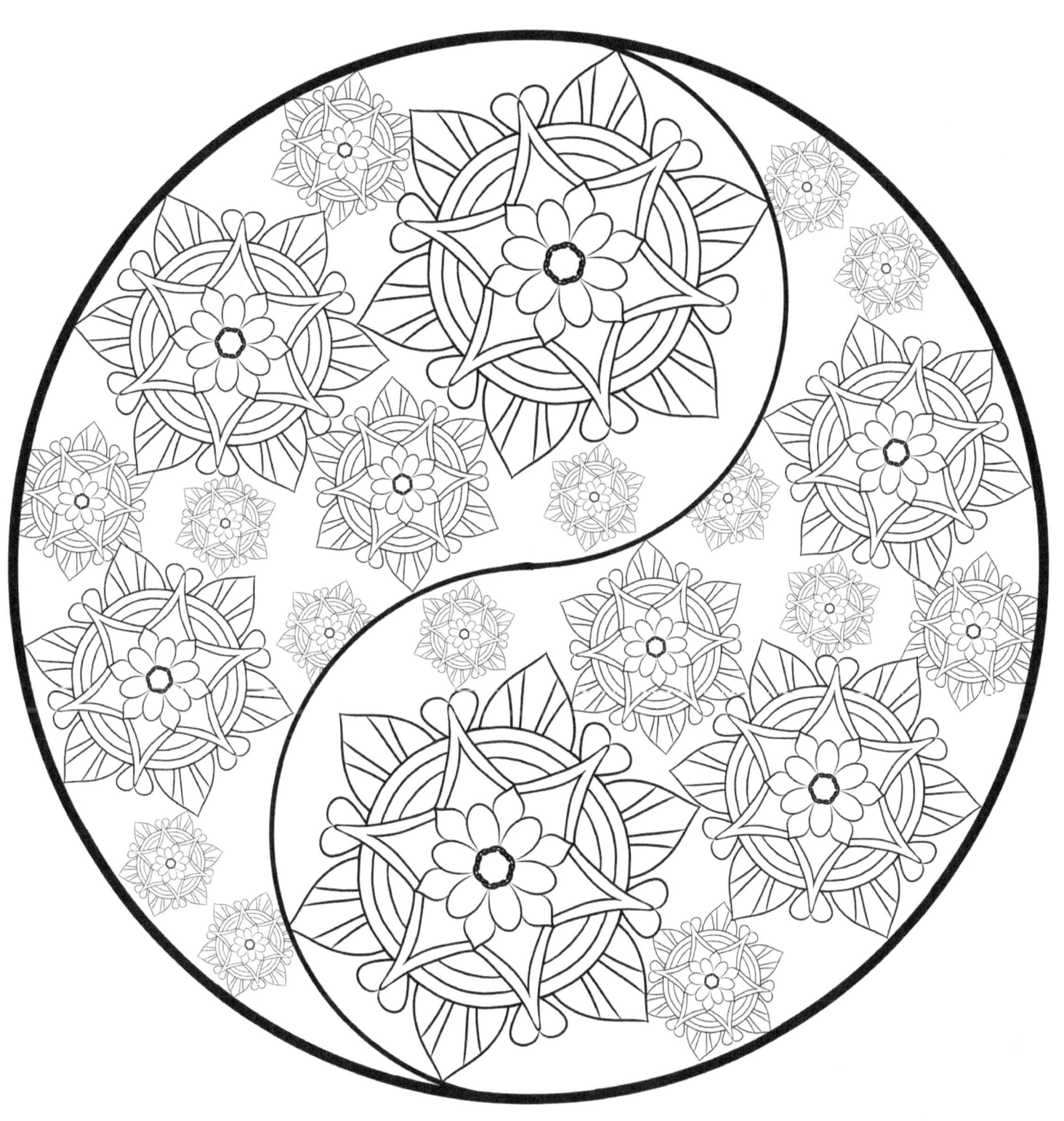

Bleed Through Barrier

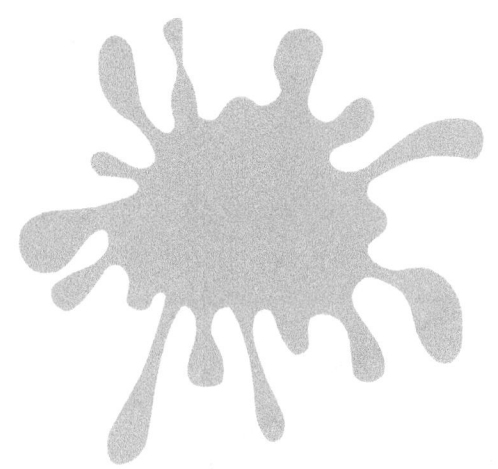

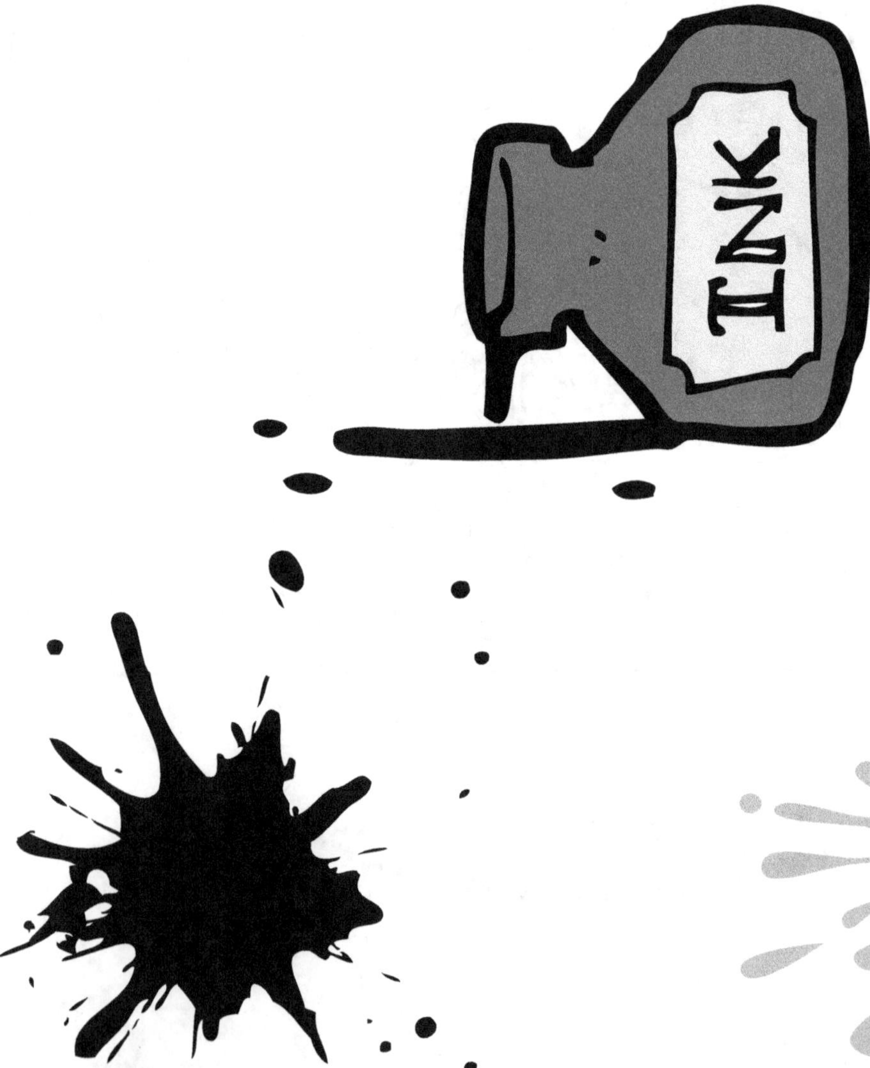

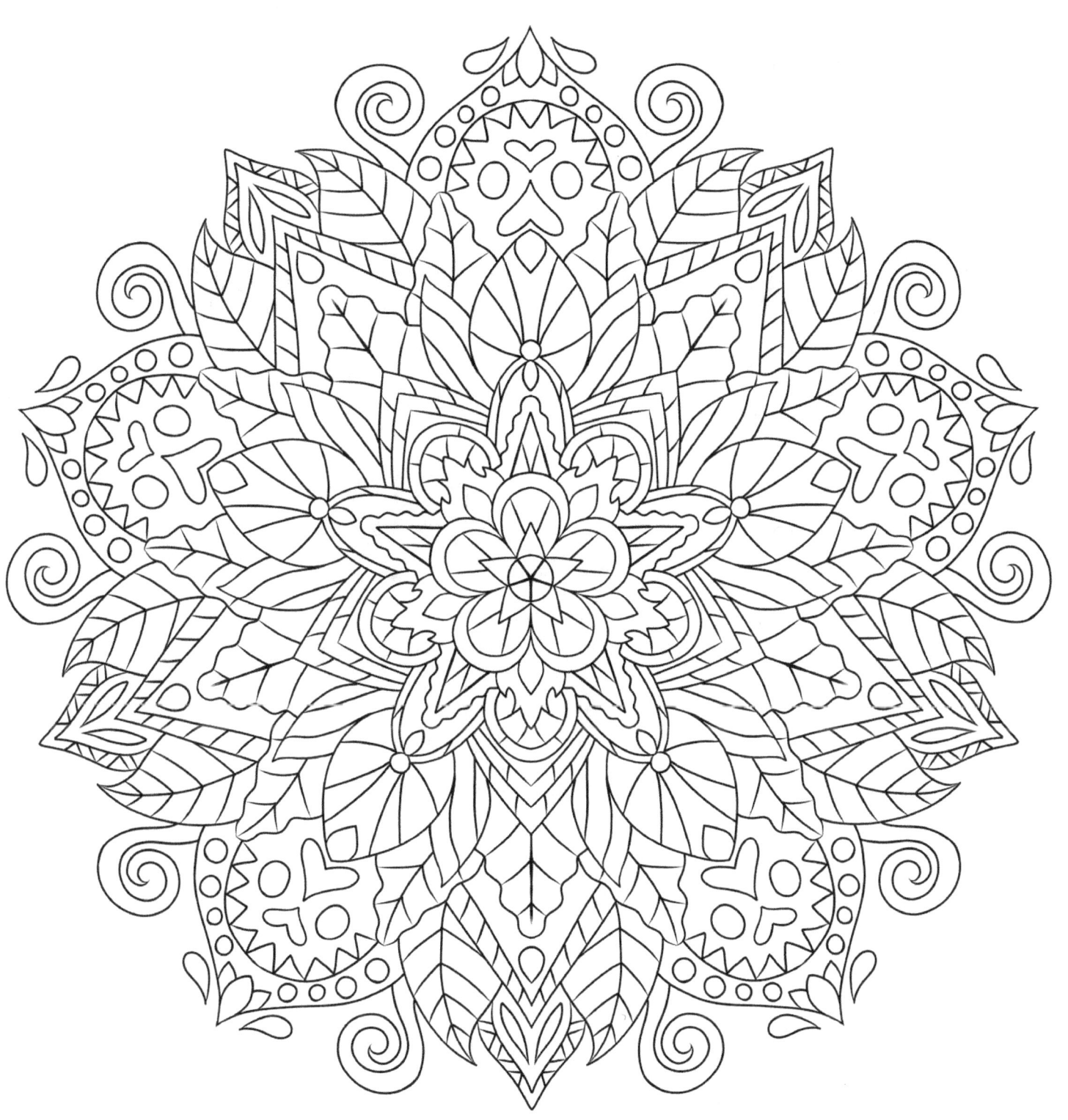

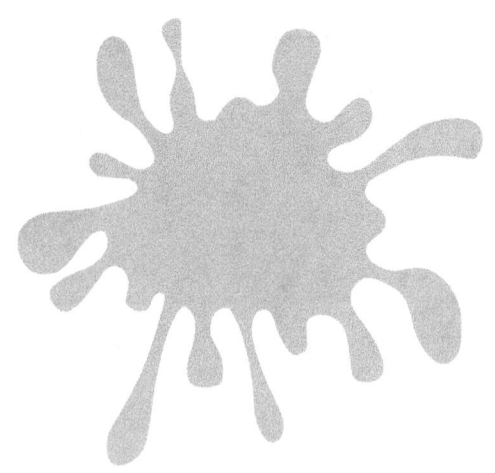

Bleed Through Barrier

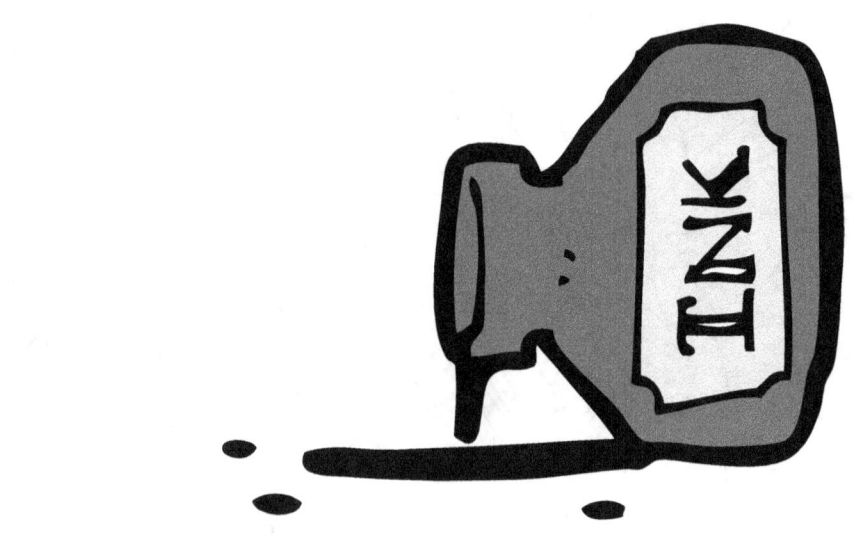

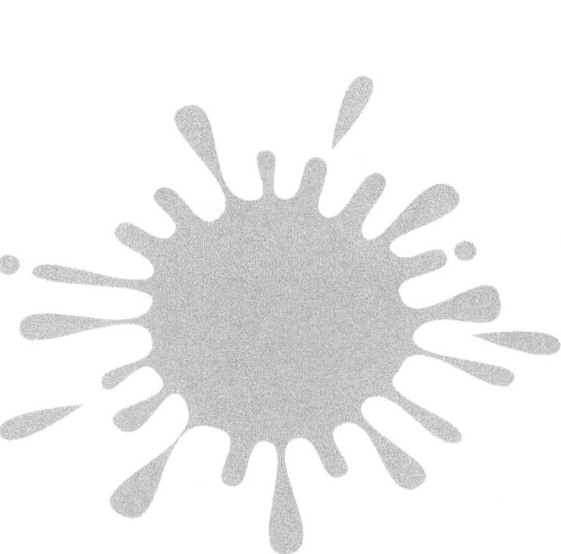

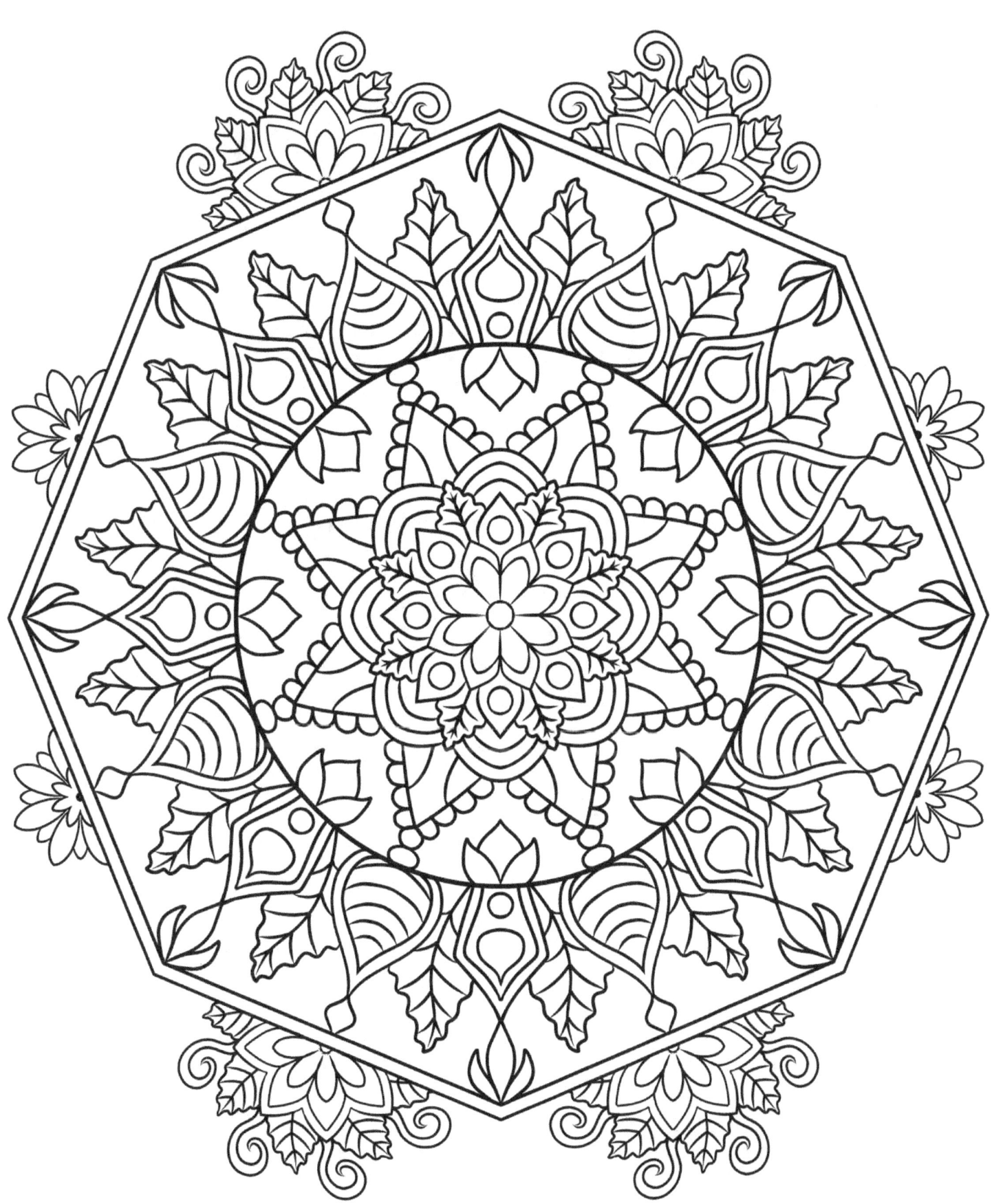

Bleed Through Barrier

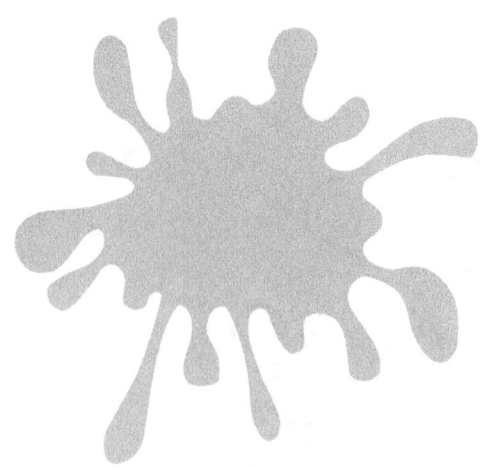

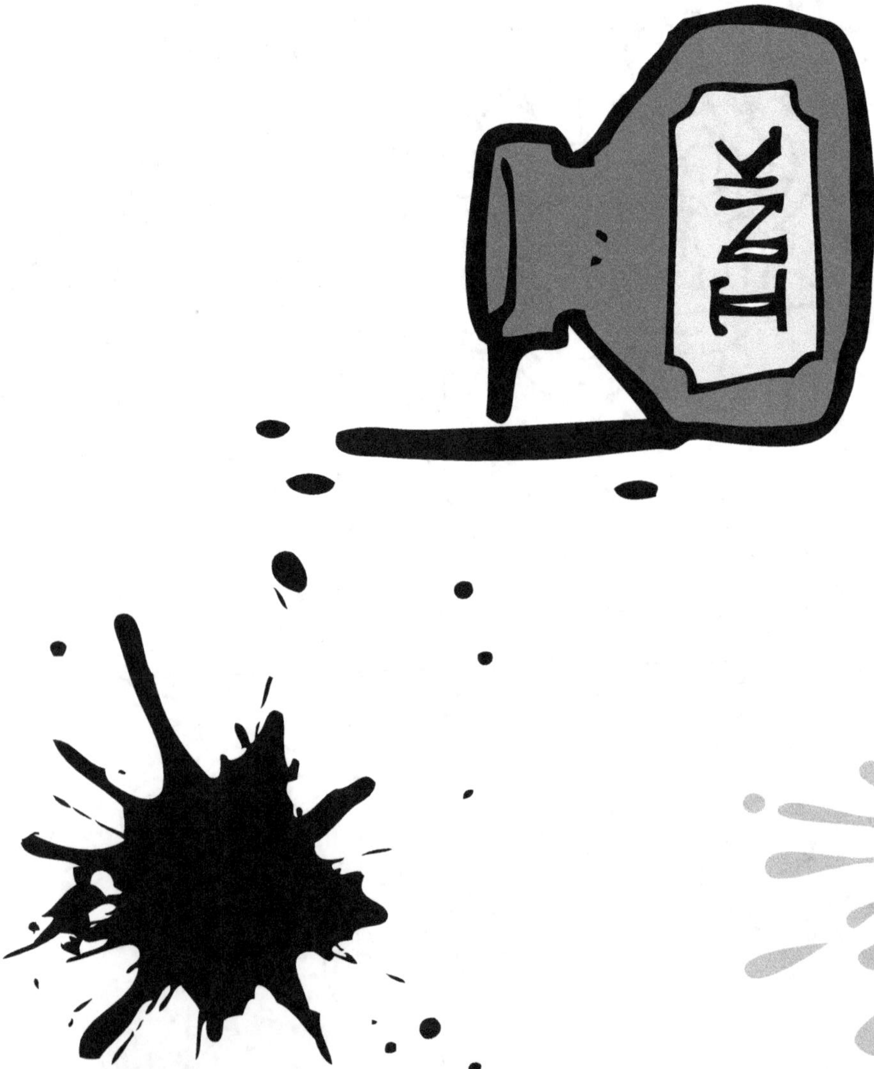

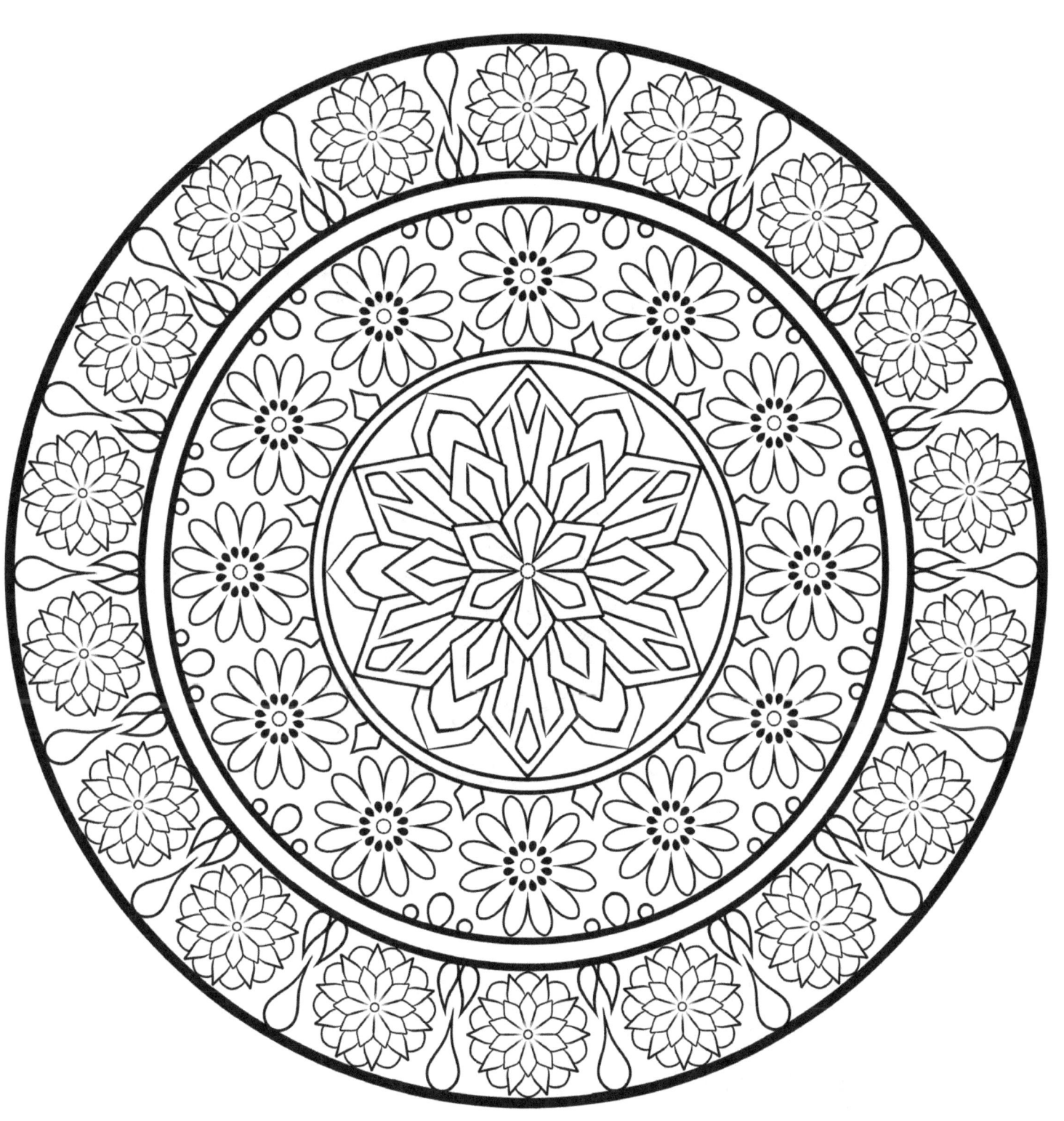

Bleed Through Barrier

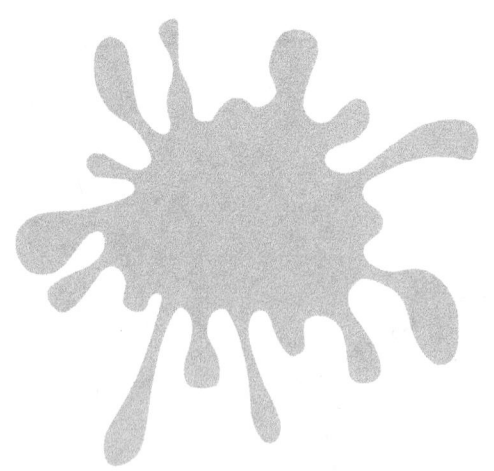

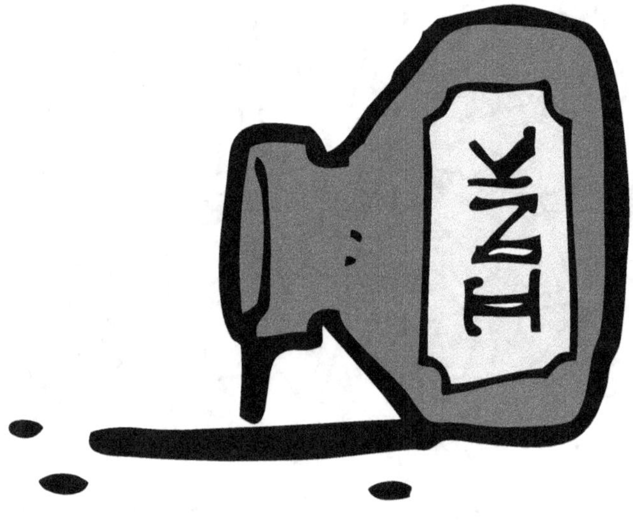

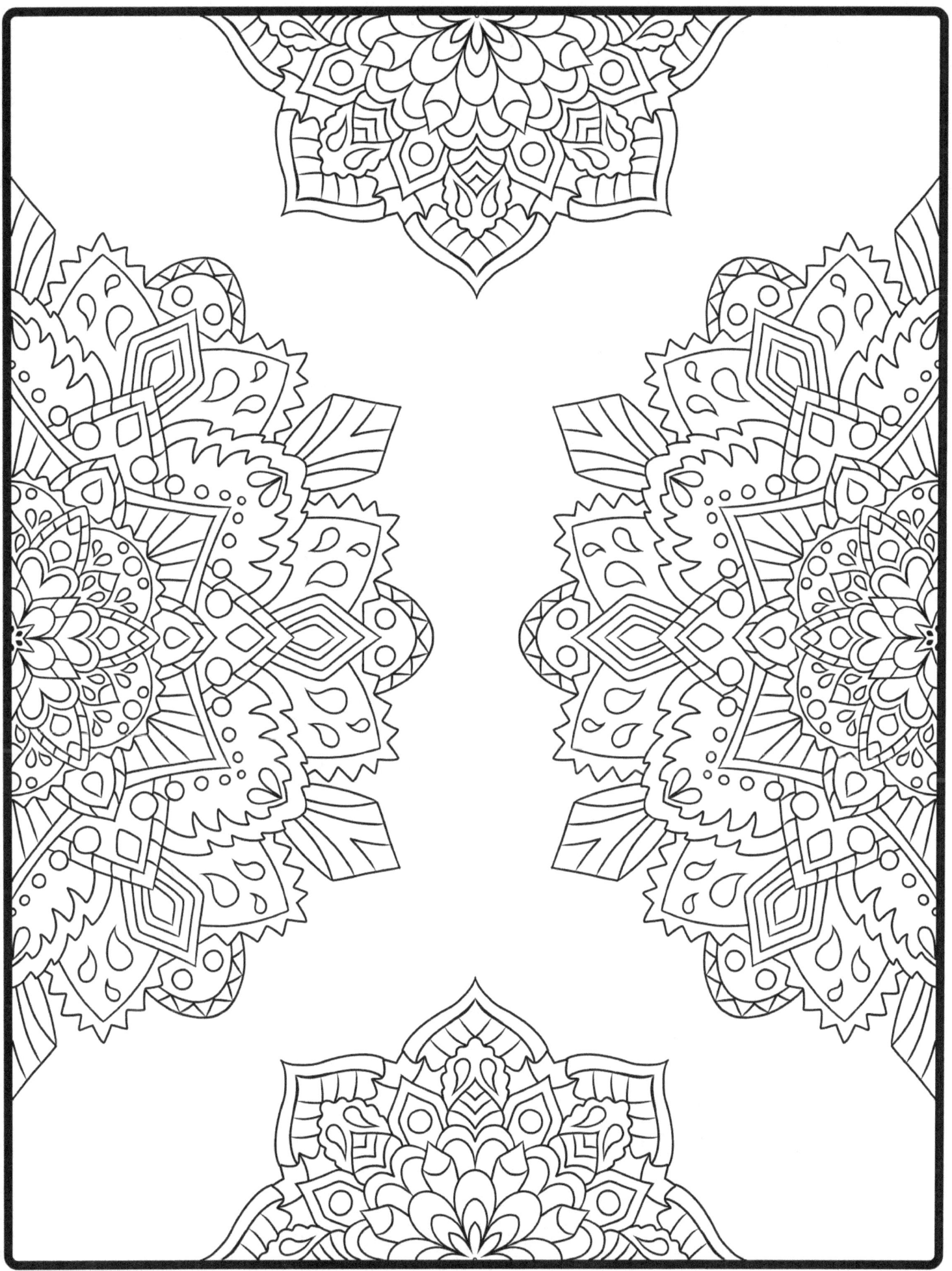

Bleed Through Barrier

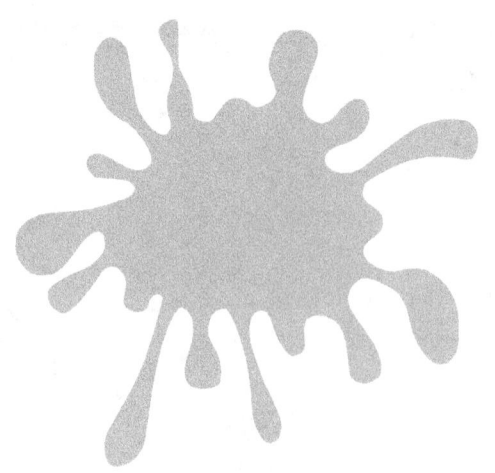

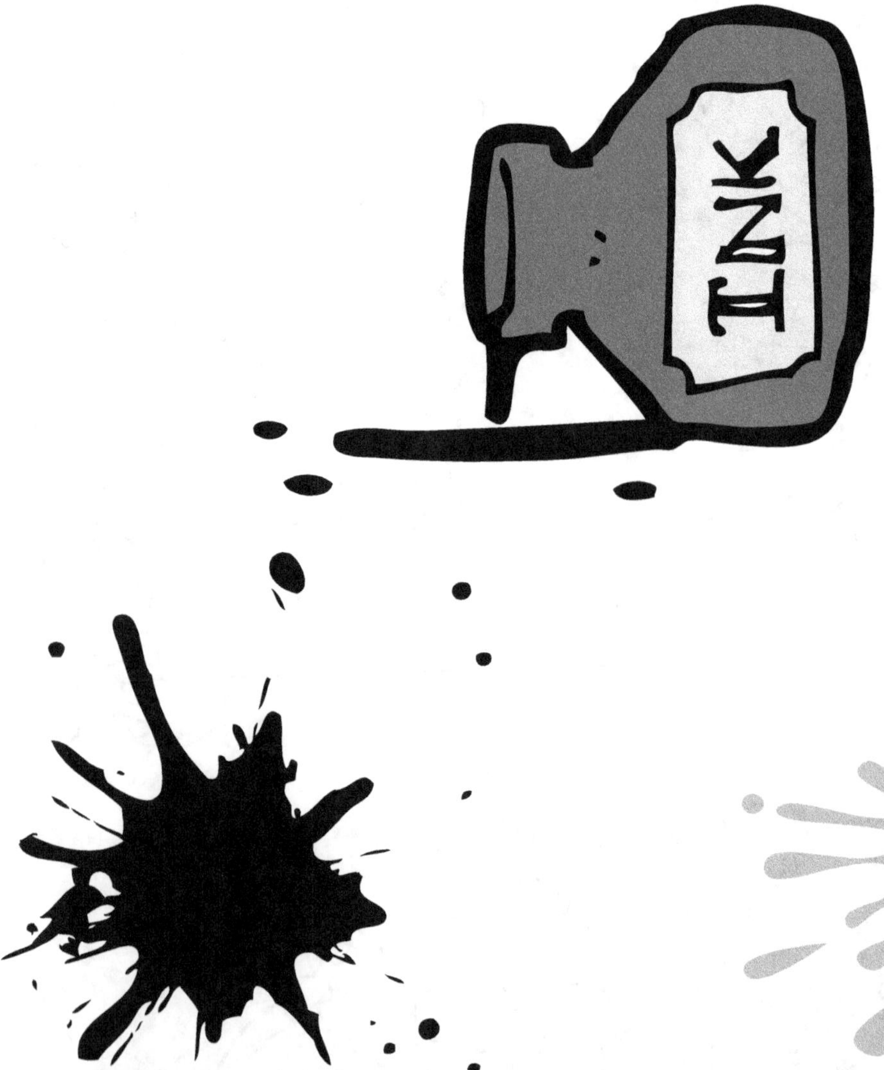

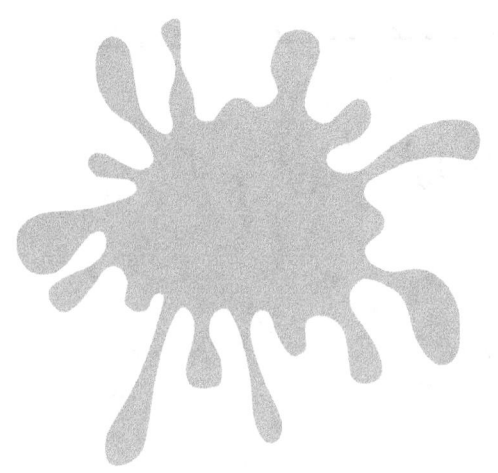

Bleed Through Barrier

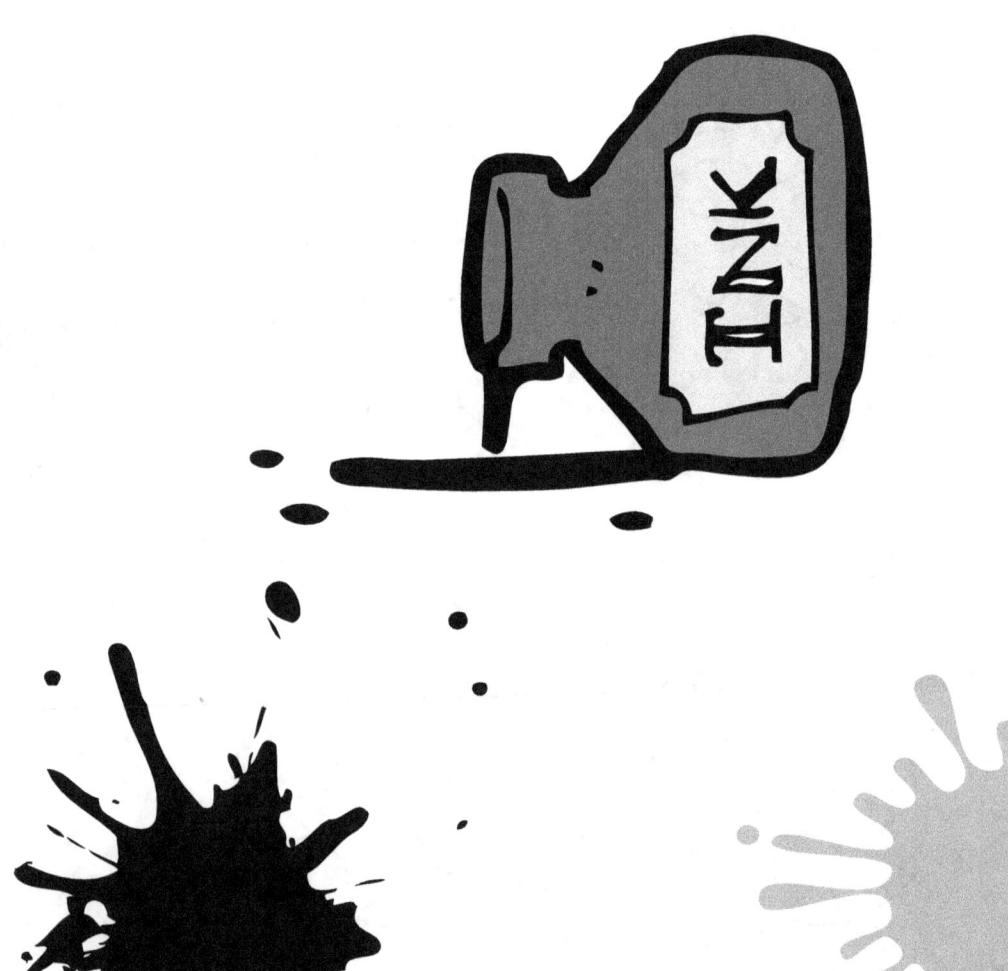

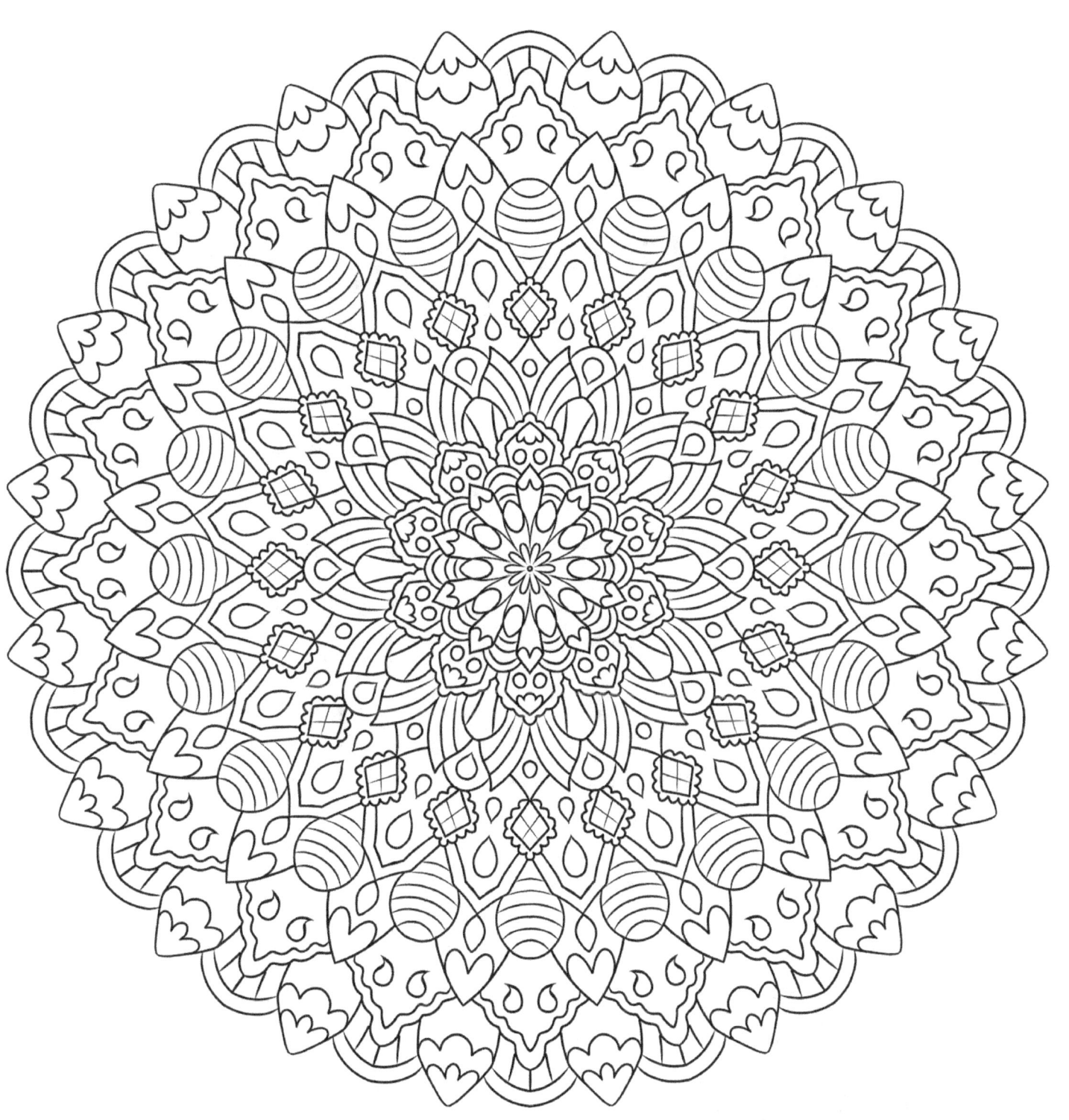

Bleed Through Barrier

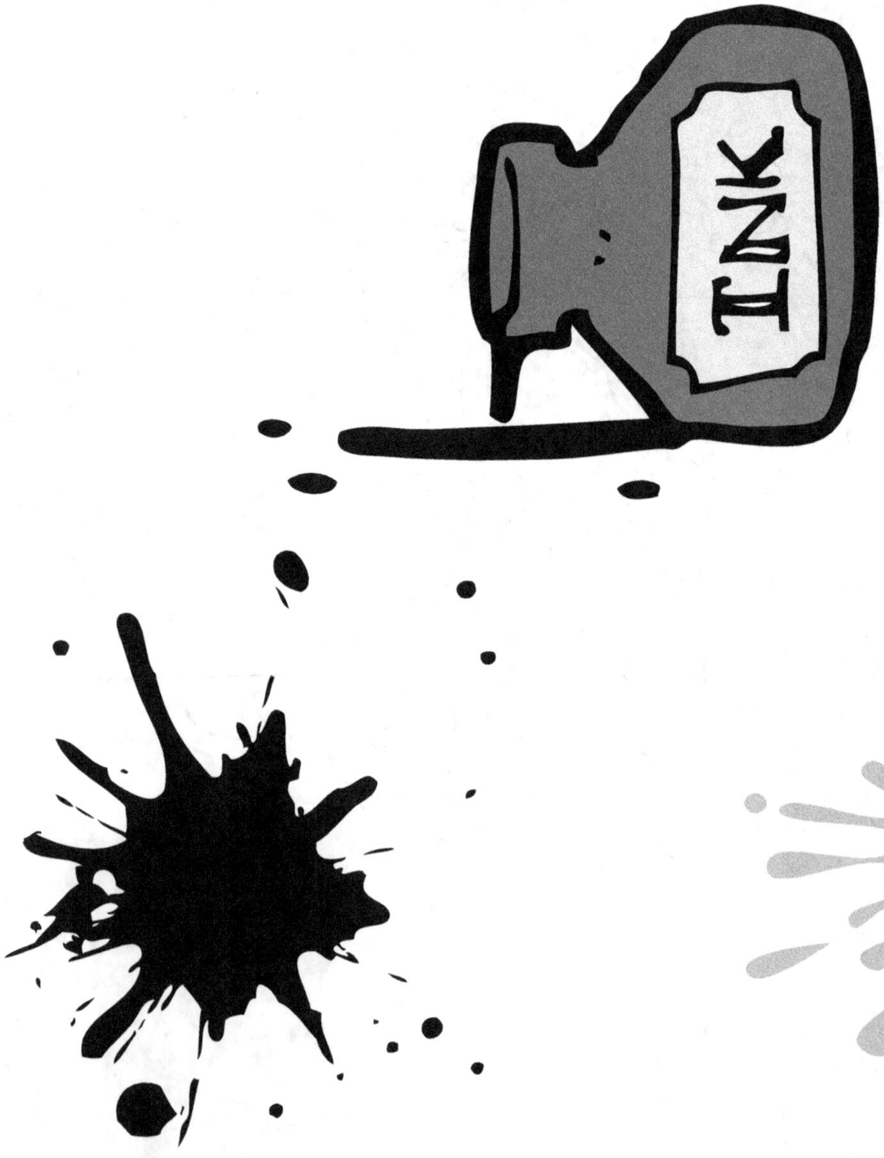

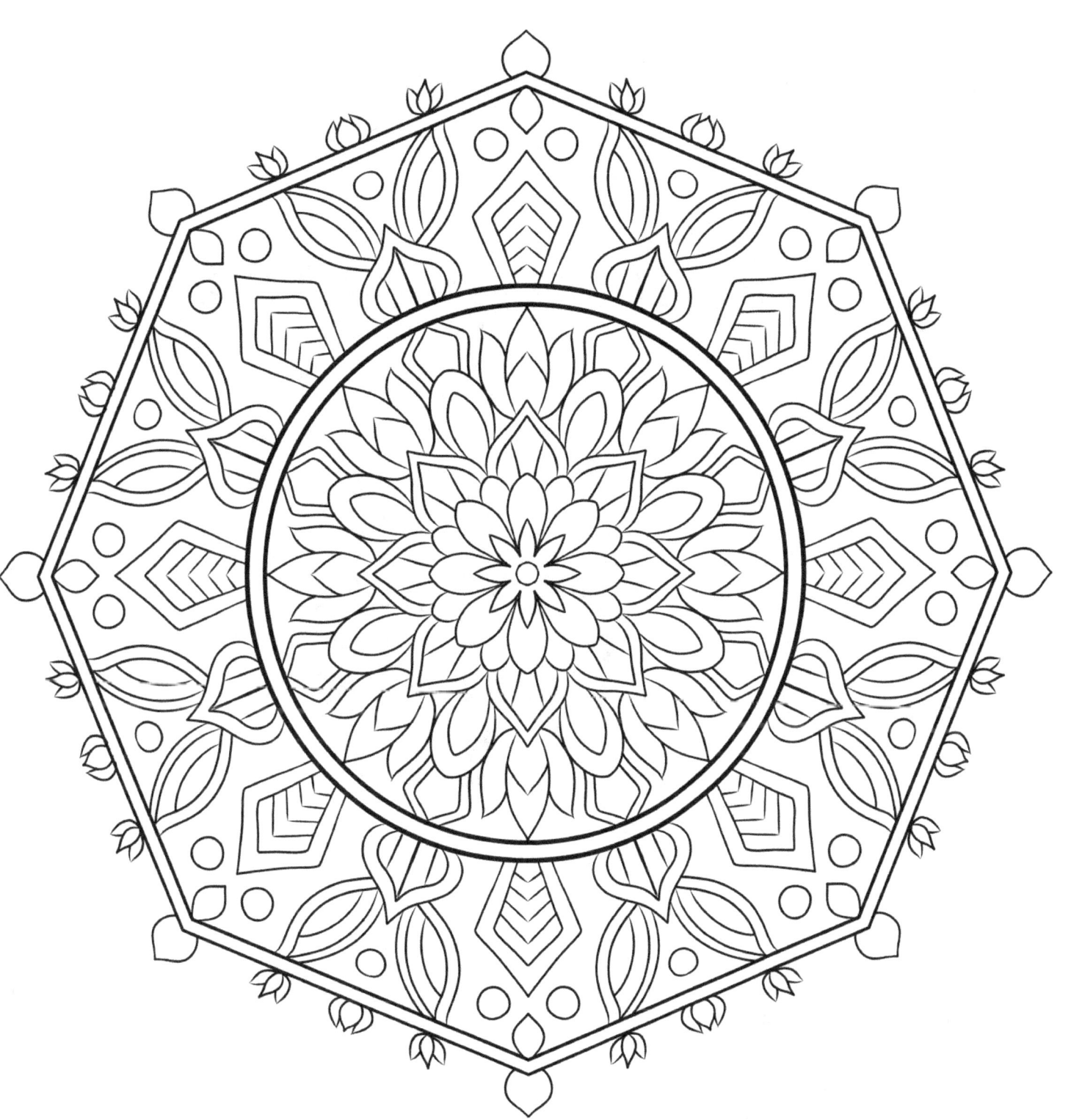

Bleed Through Barrier

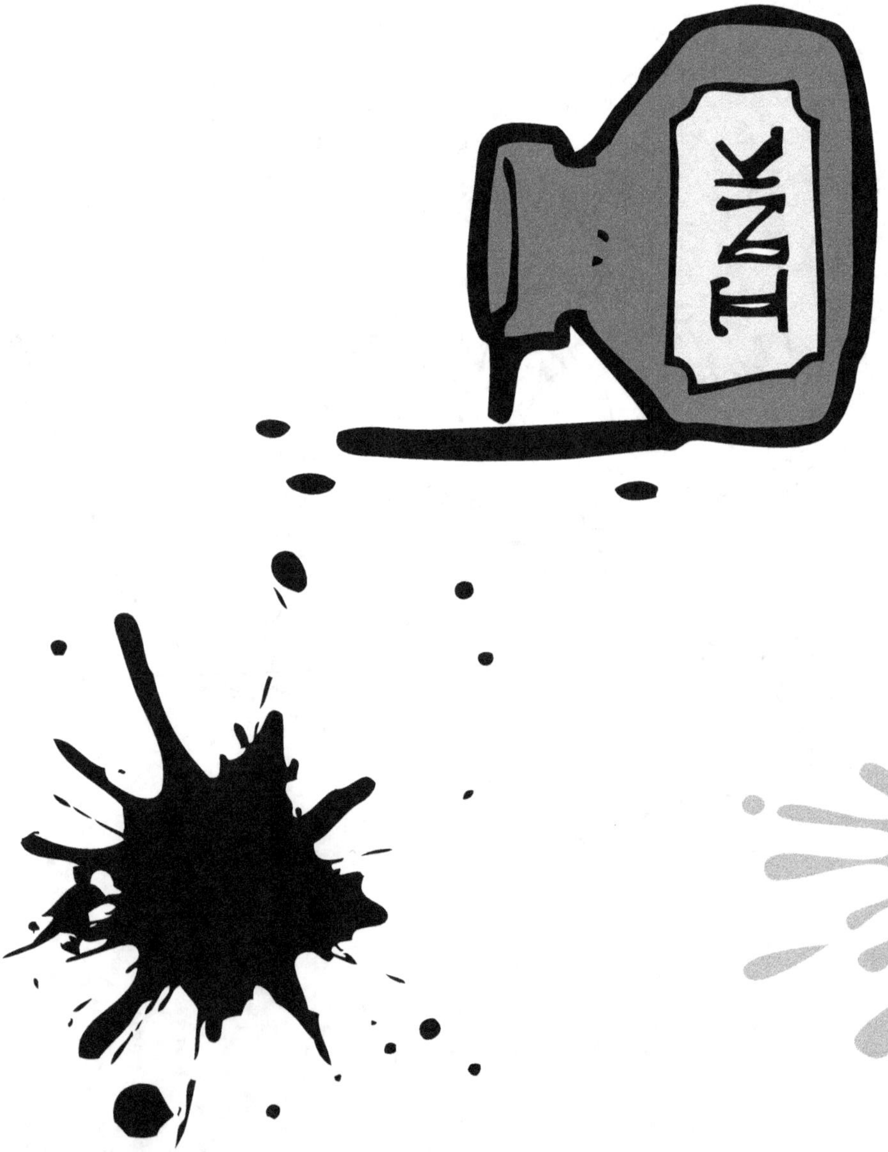

Bleed Through Barrier

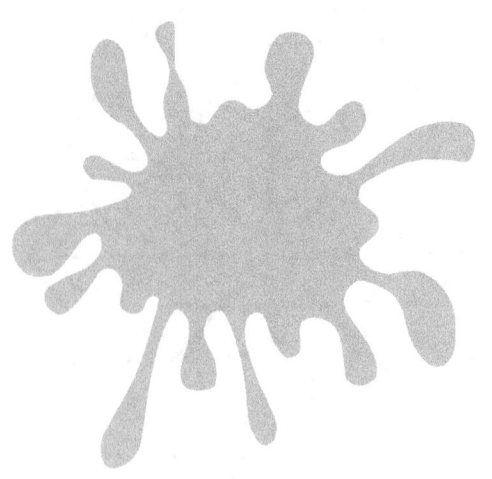

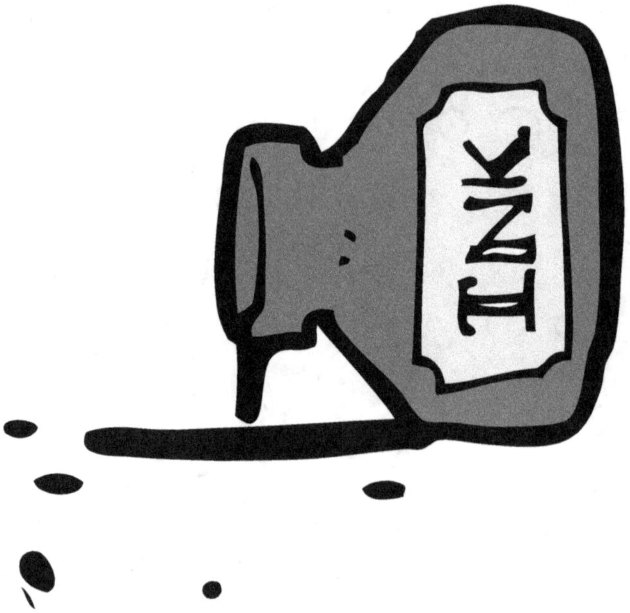

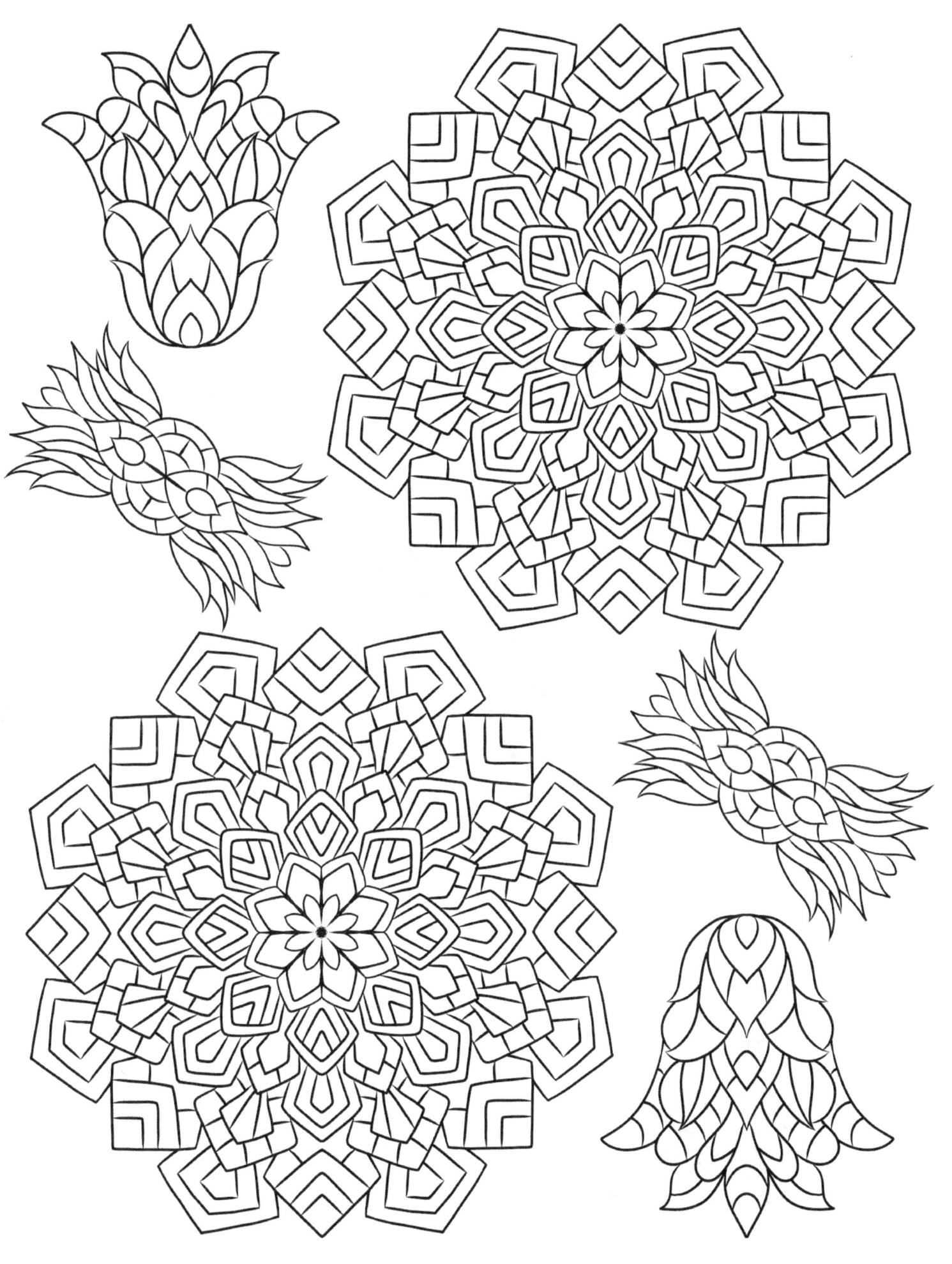

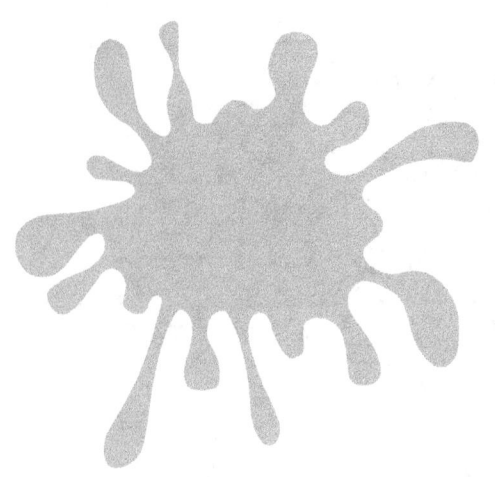

Bleed Through Barrier

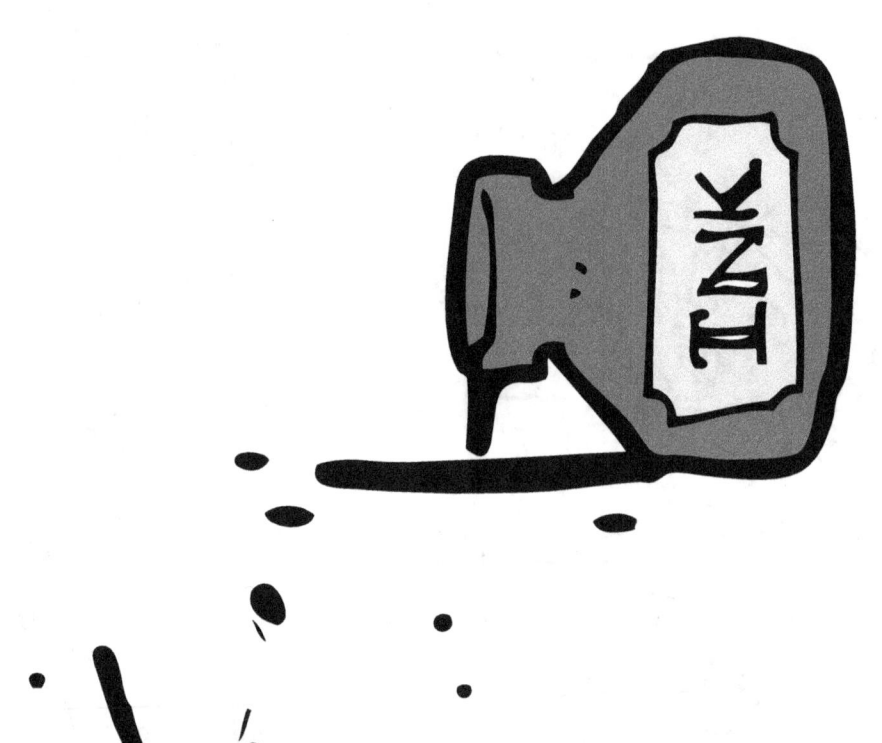

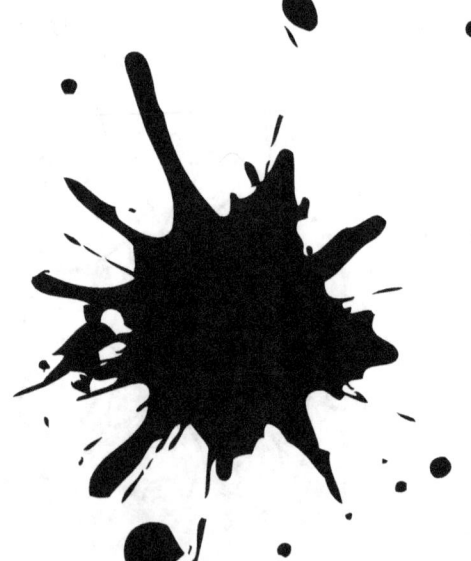

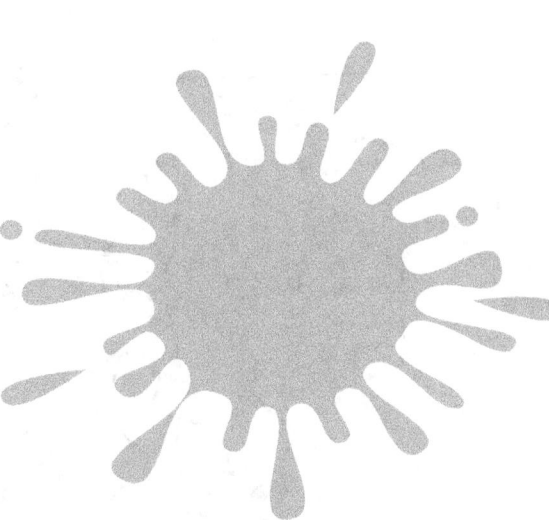

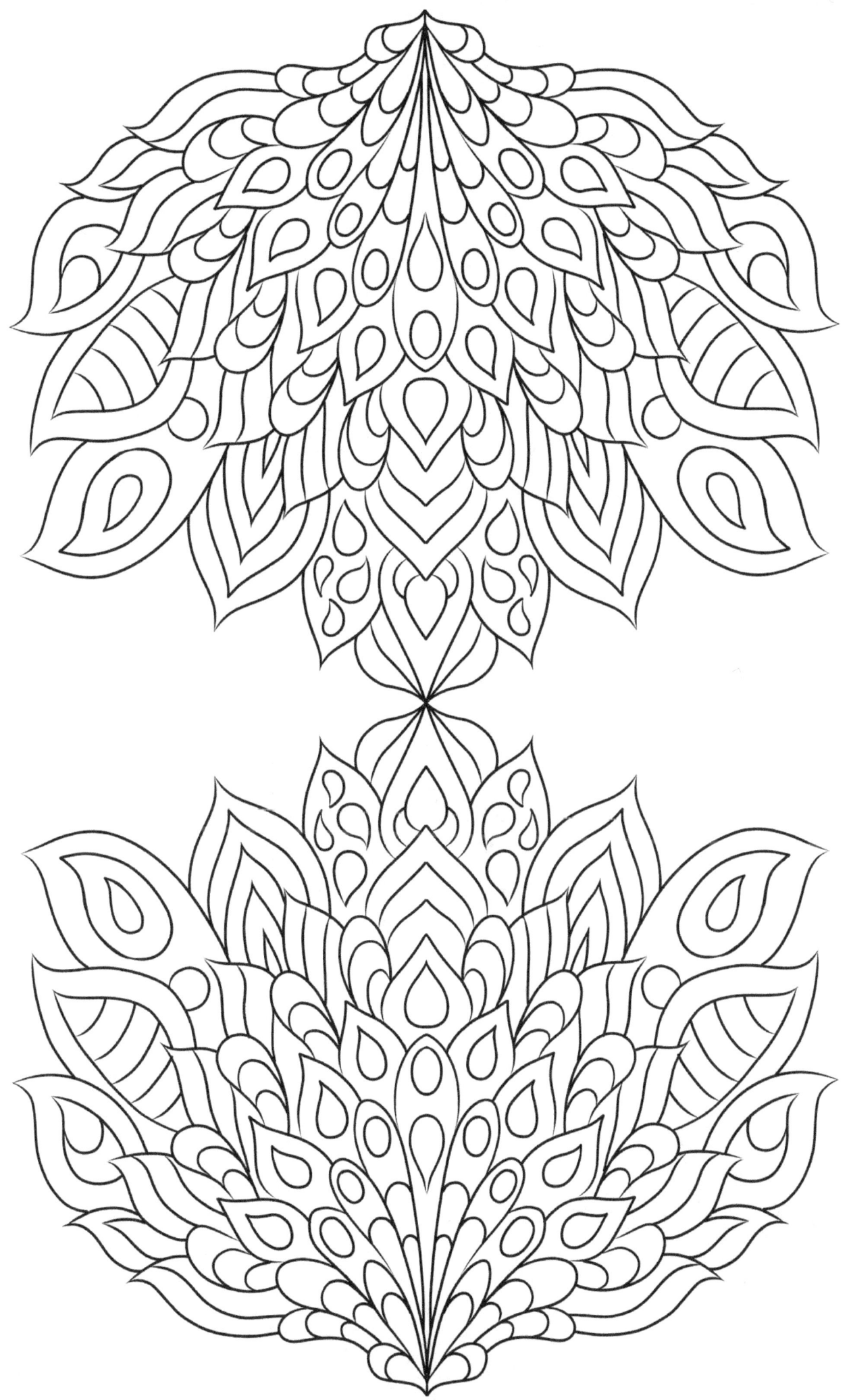

Bleed Through Barrier

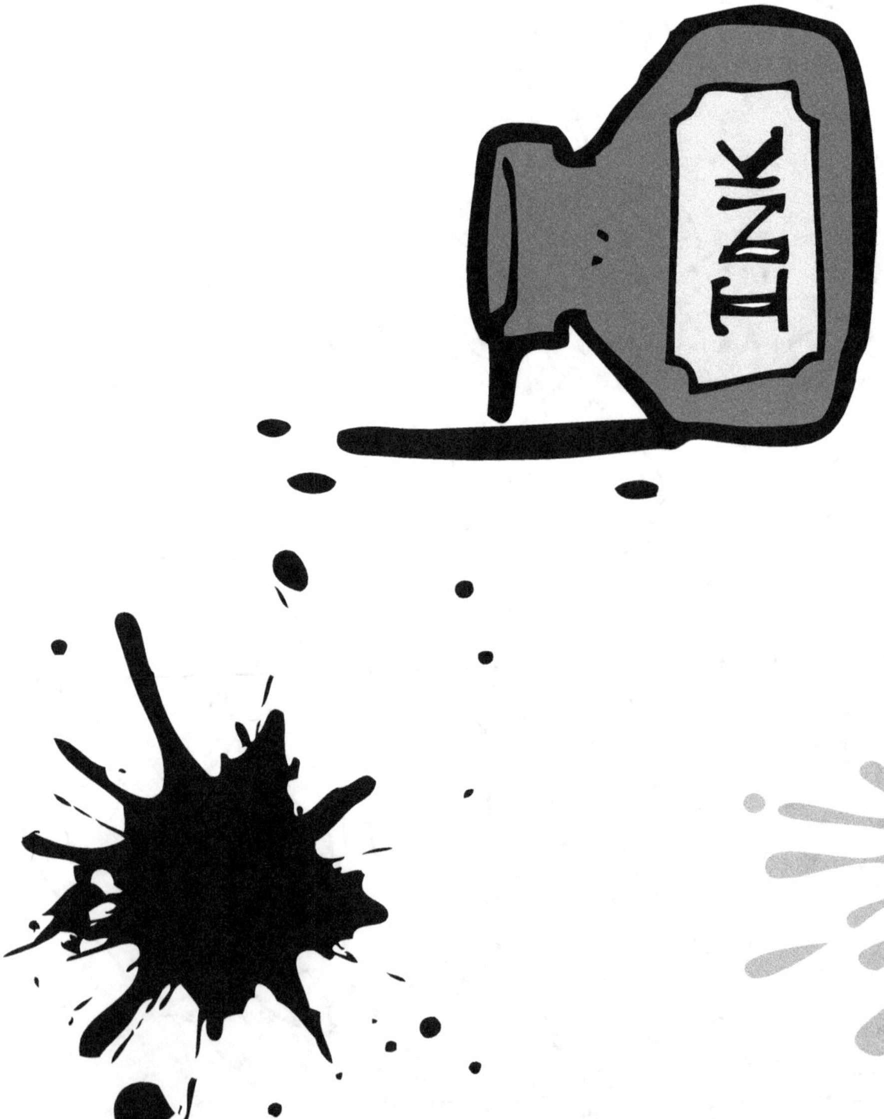

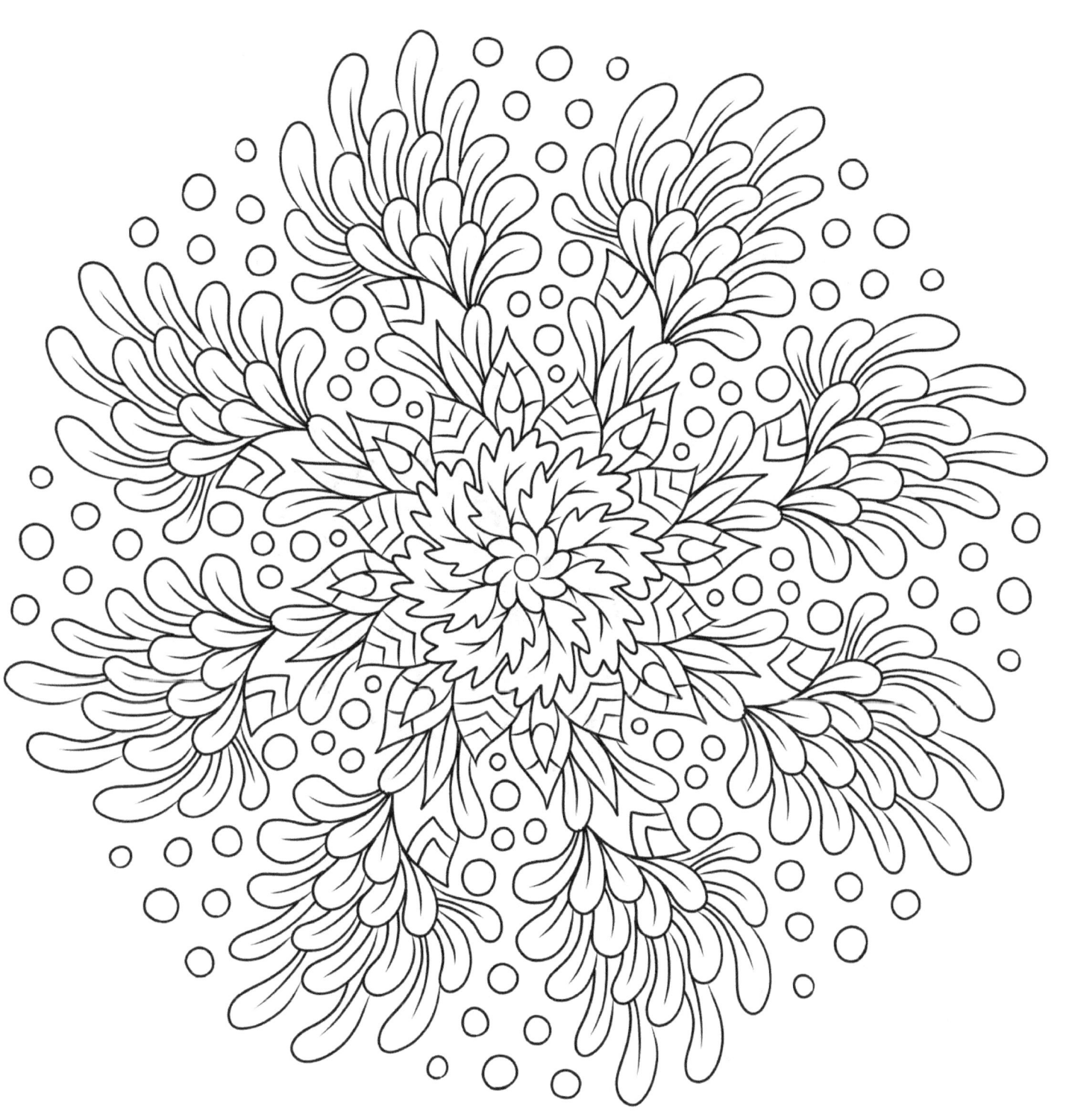

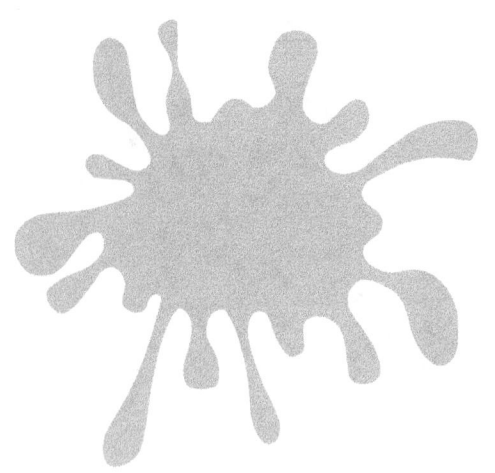

Bleed Through Barrier

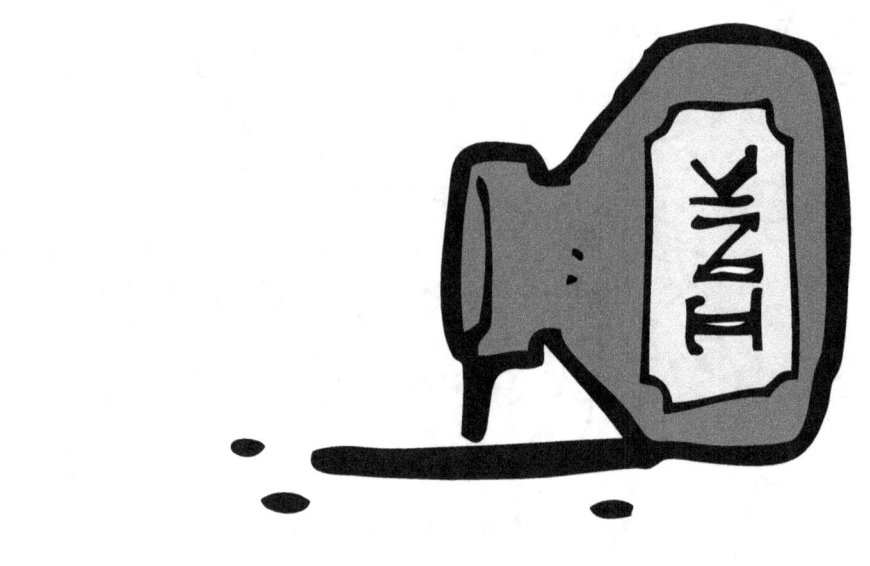

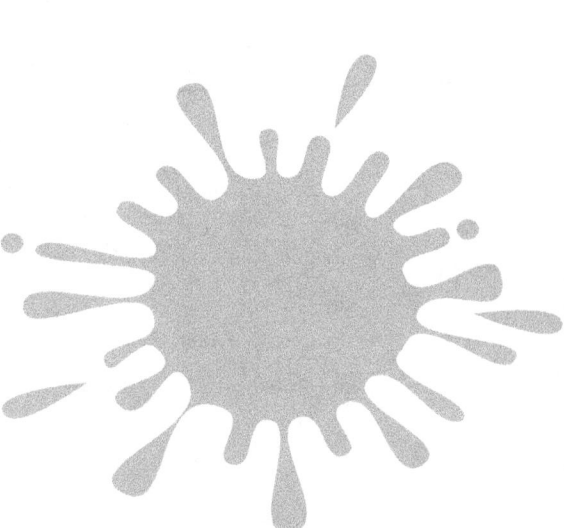

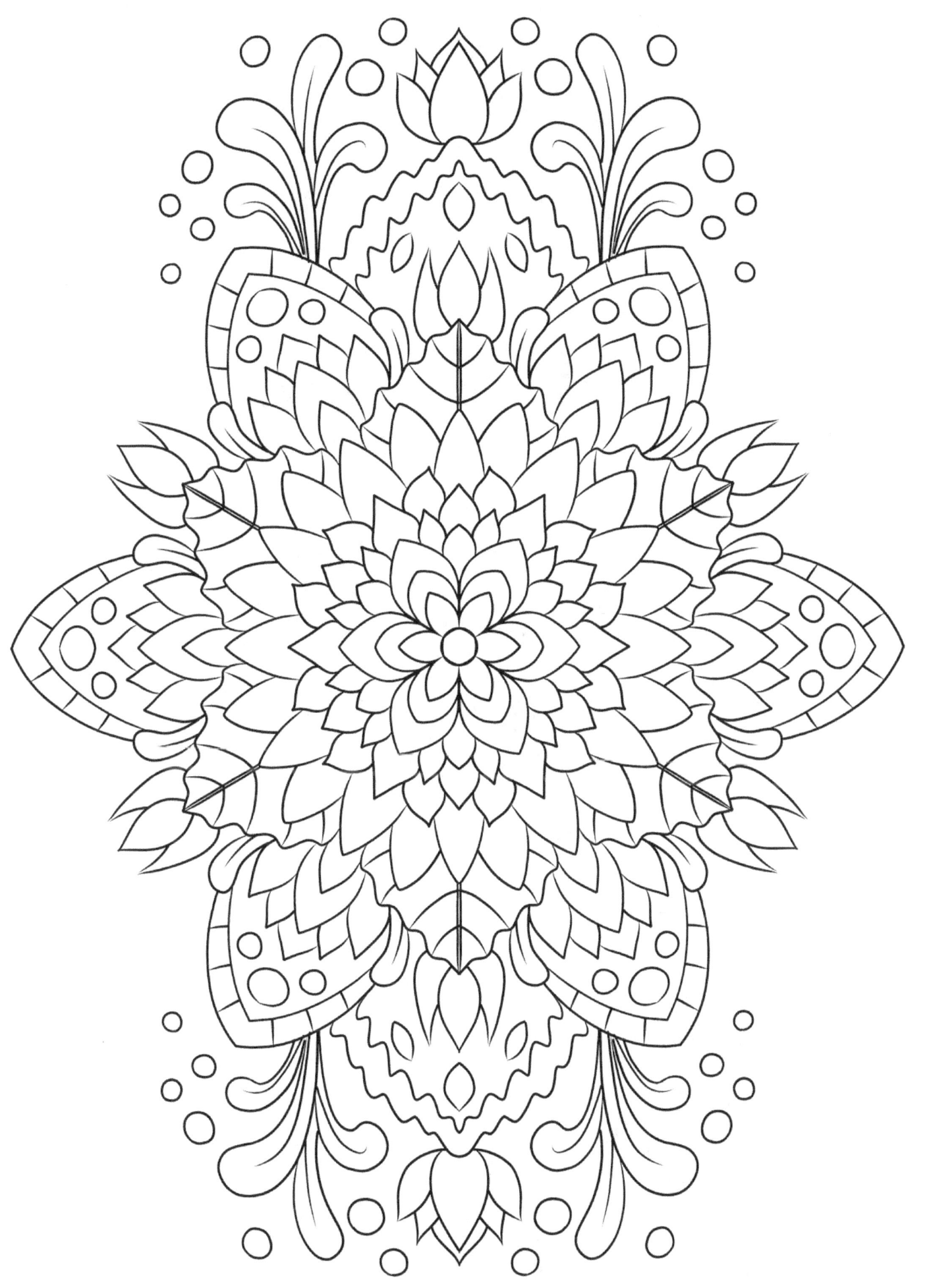

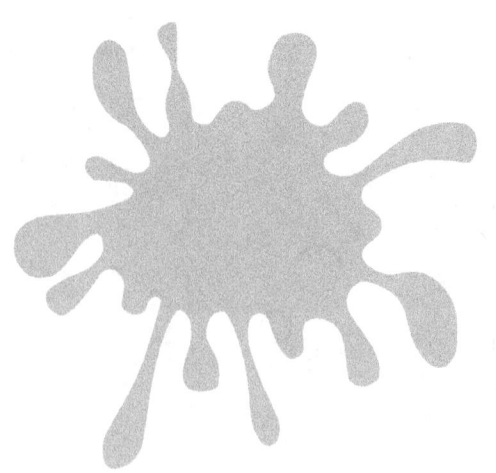

Bleed Through Barrier

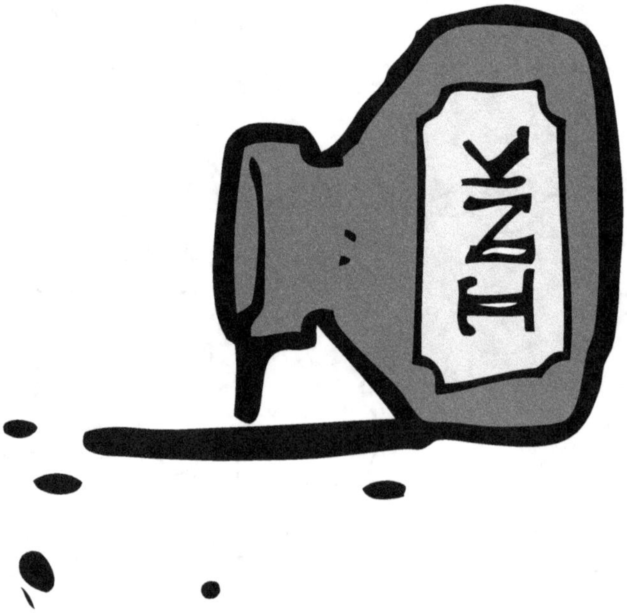

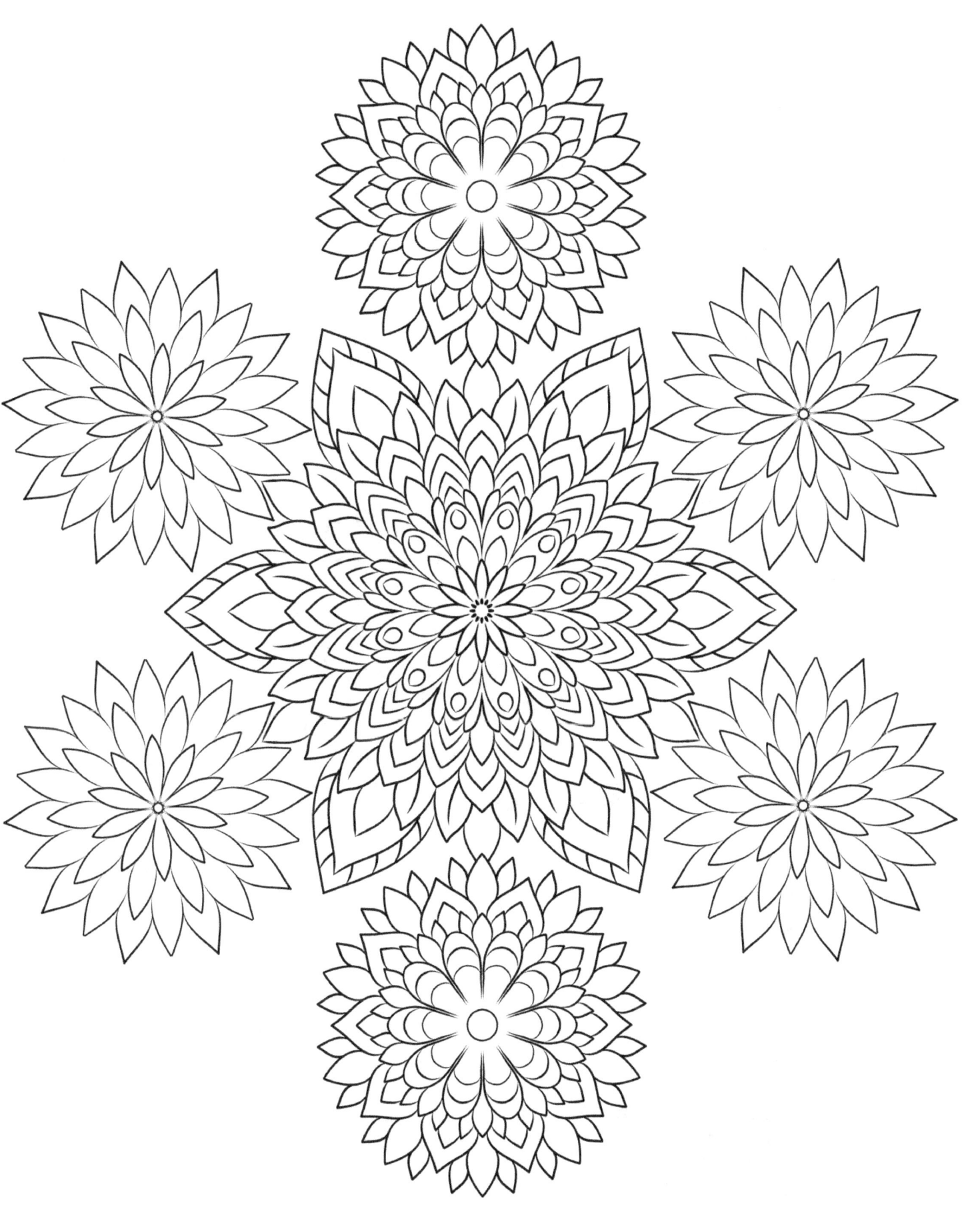

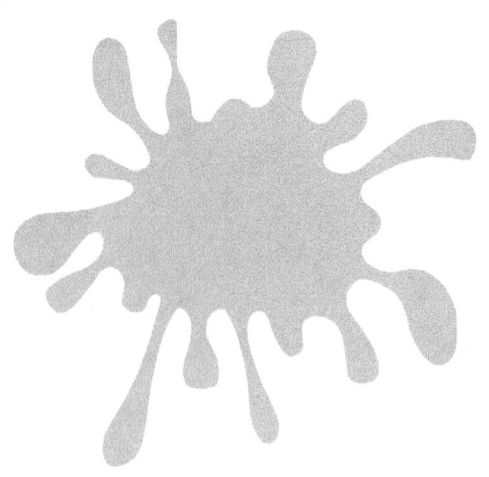

Bleed Through Barrier

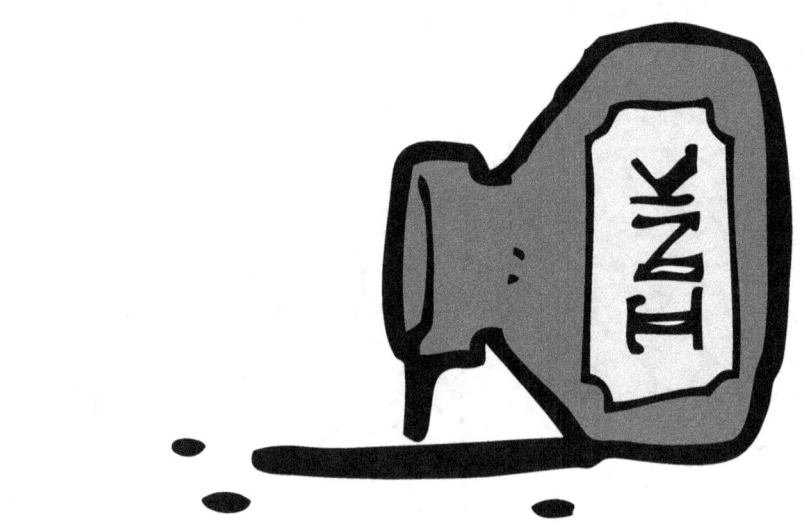

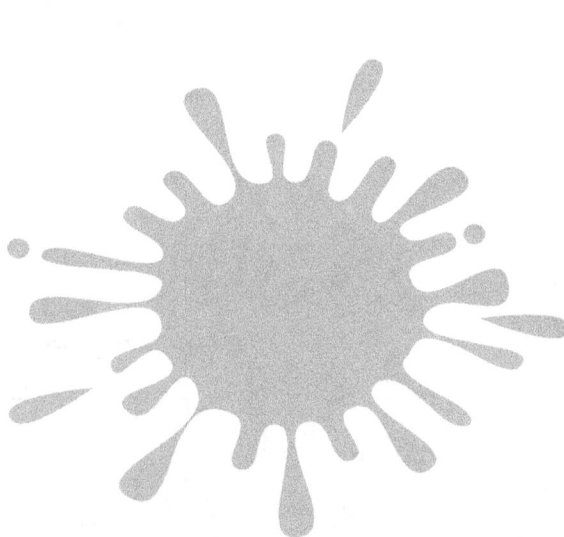

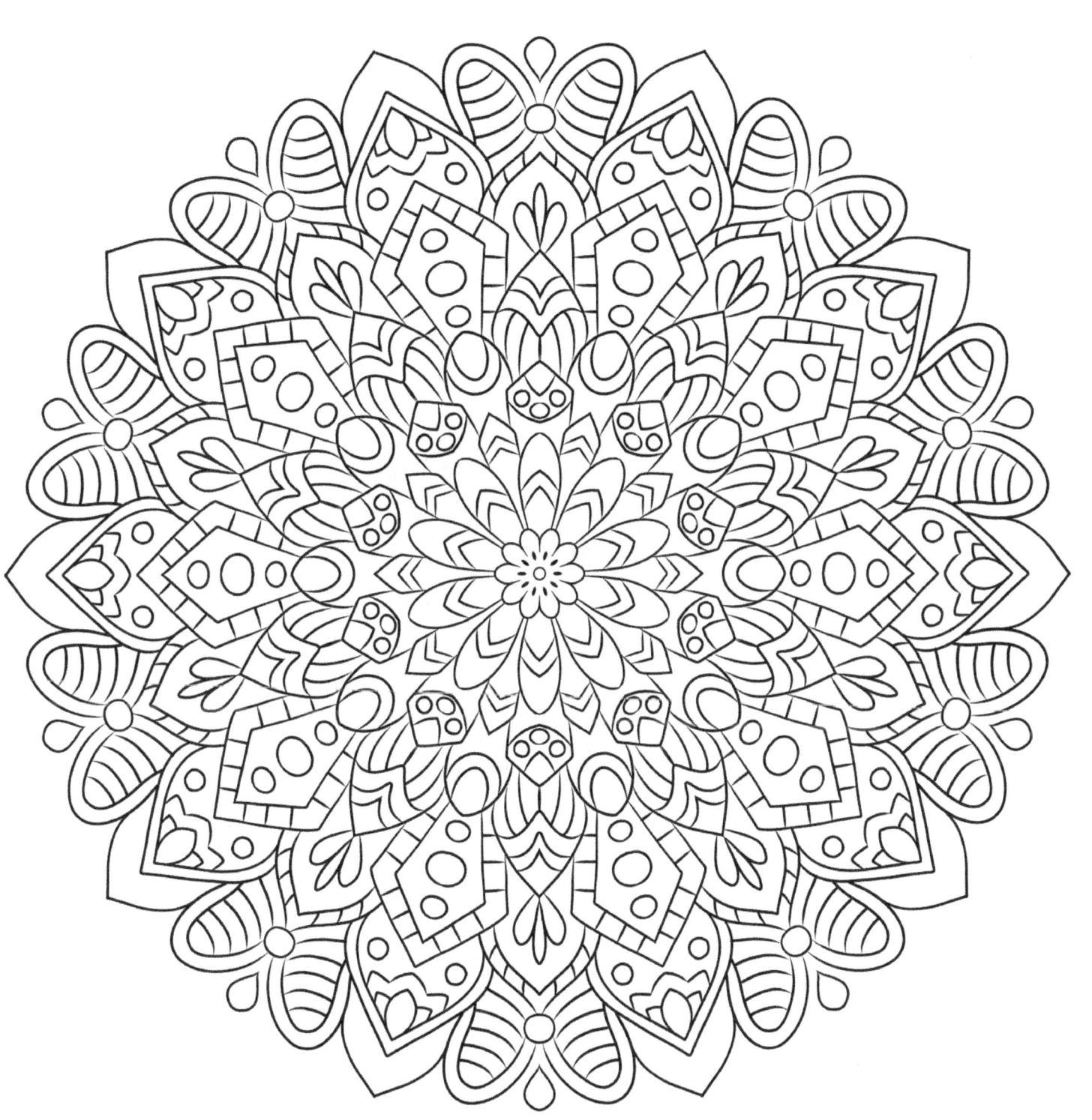

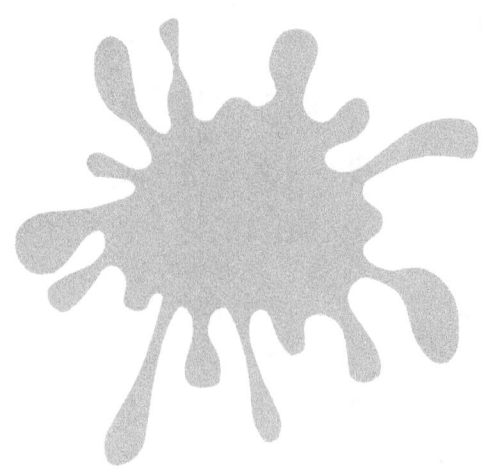

Bleed Through Barrier

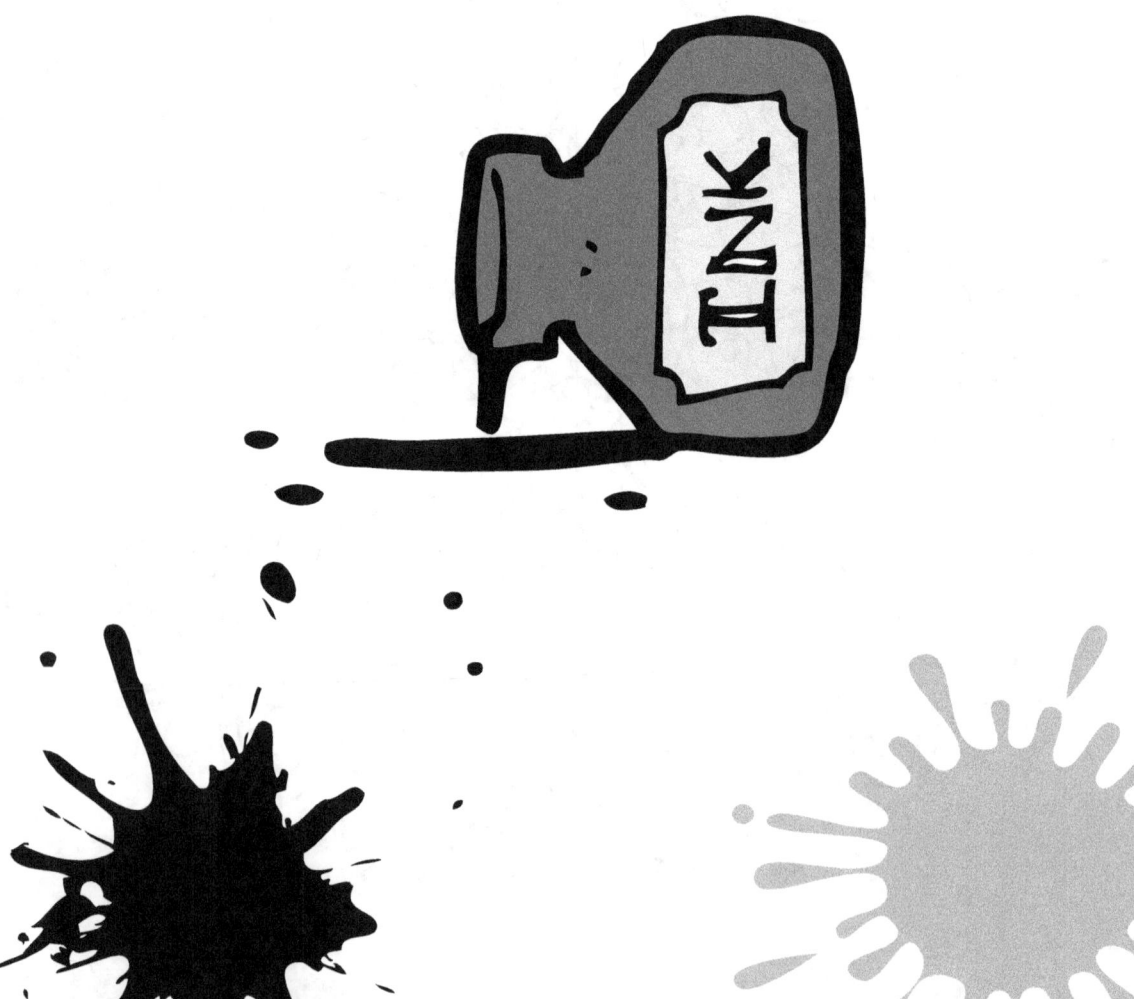

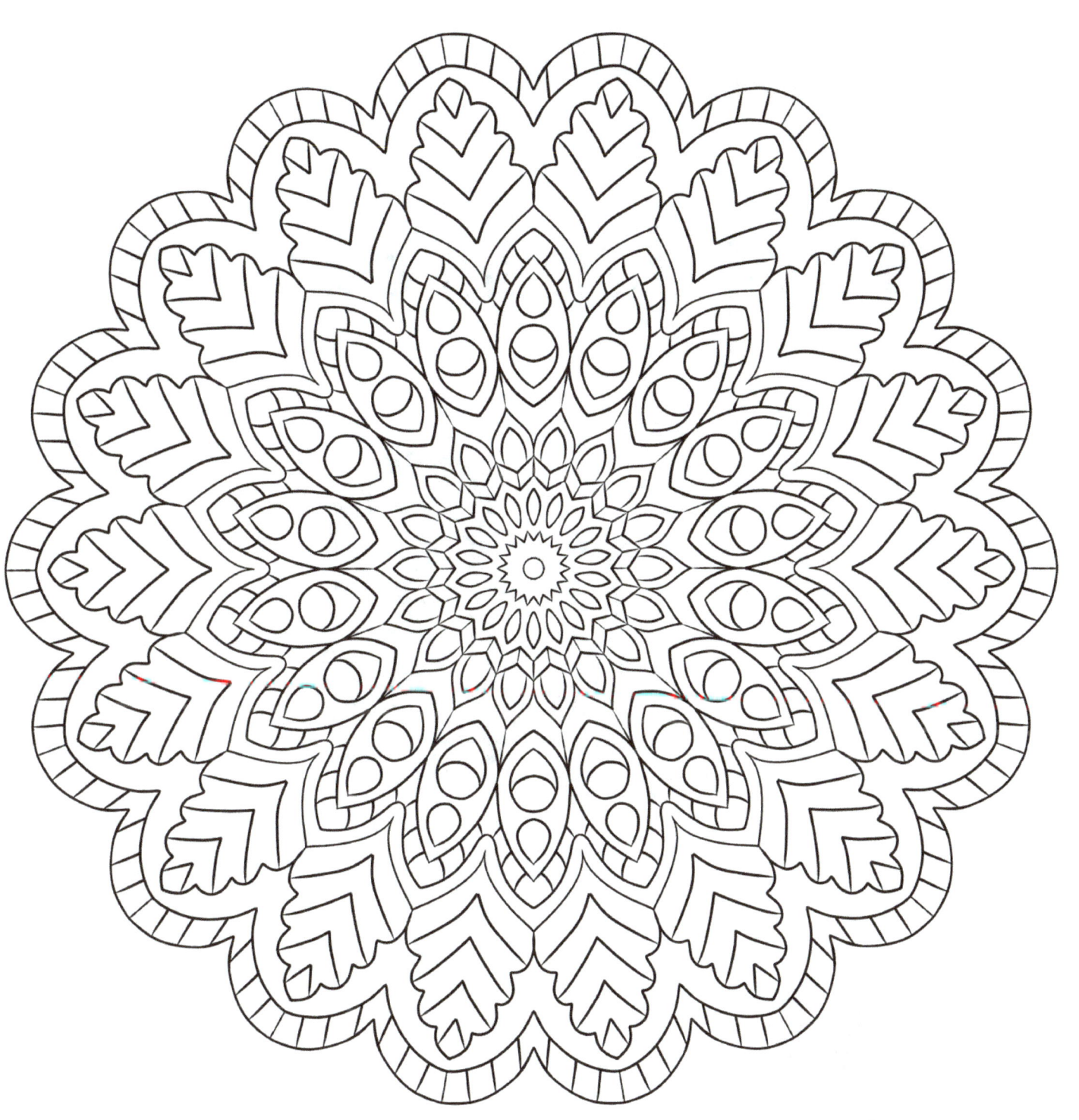

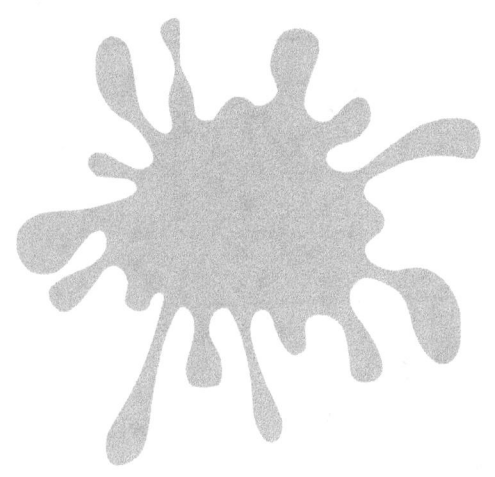

Bleed Through Barrier

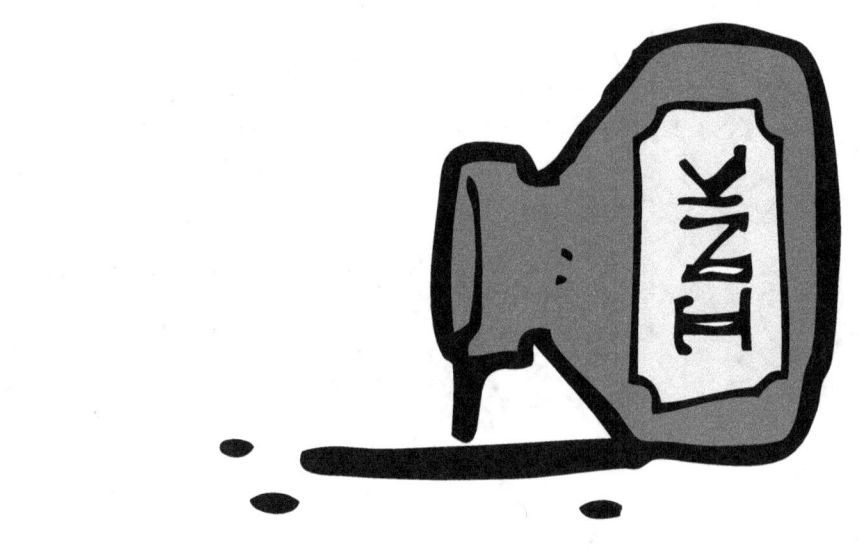

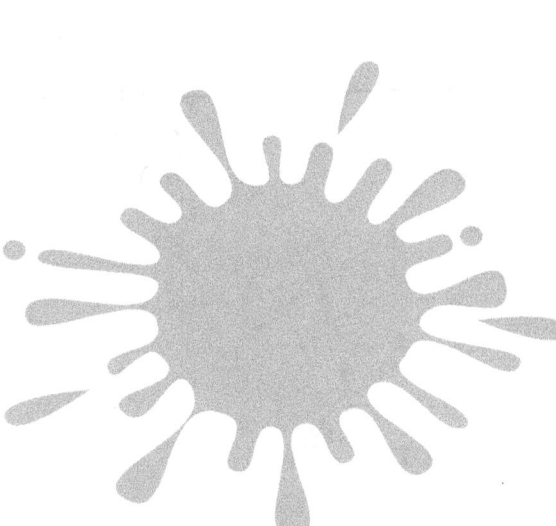

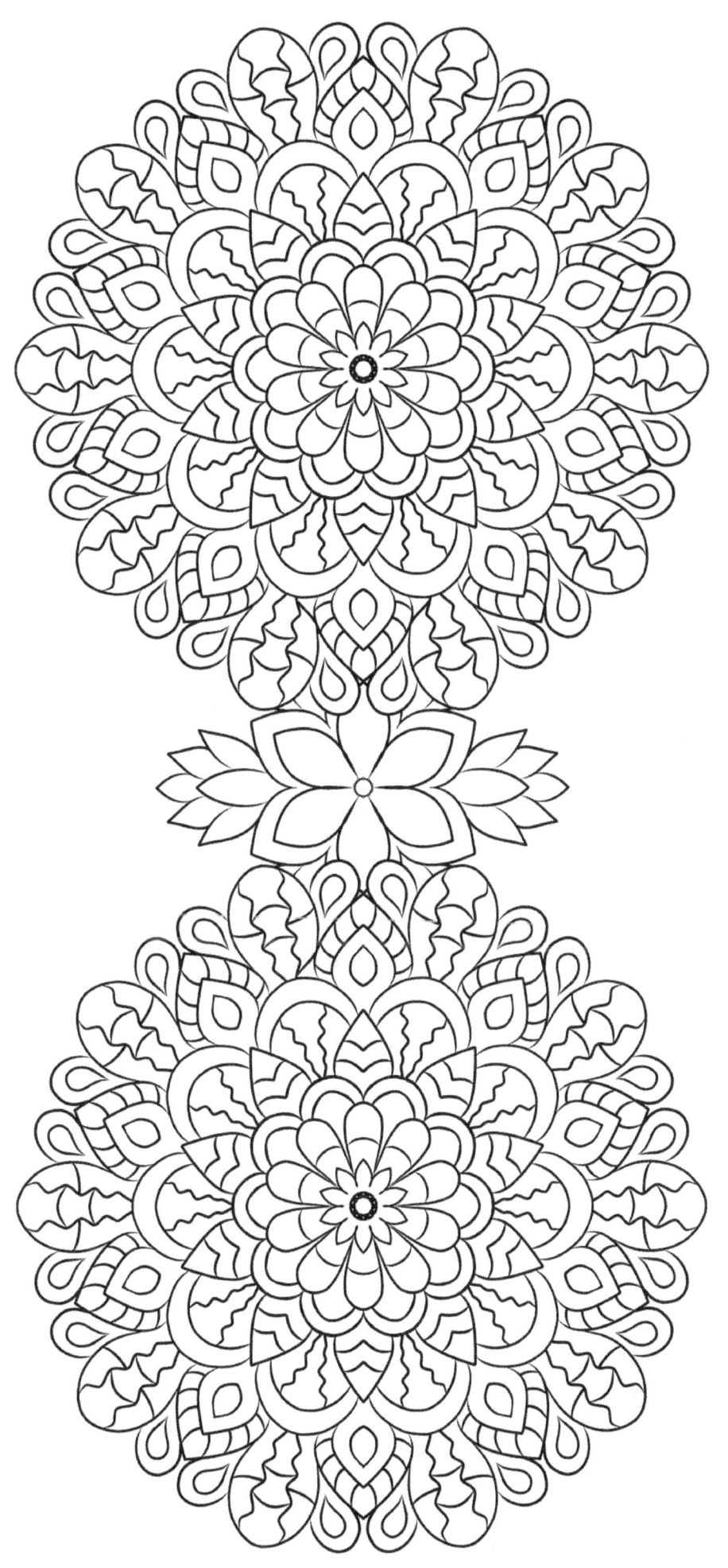

Bleed Through Barrier

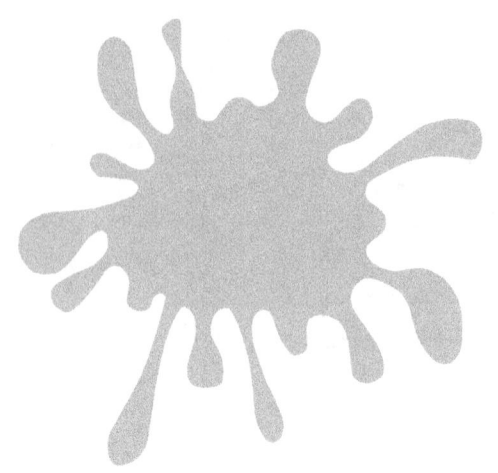

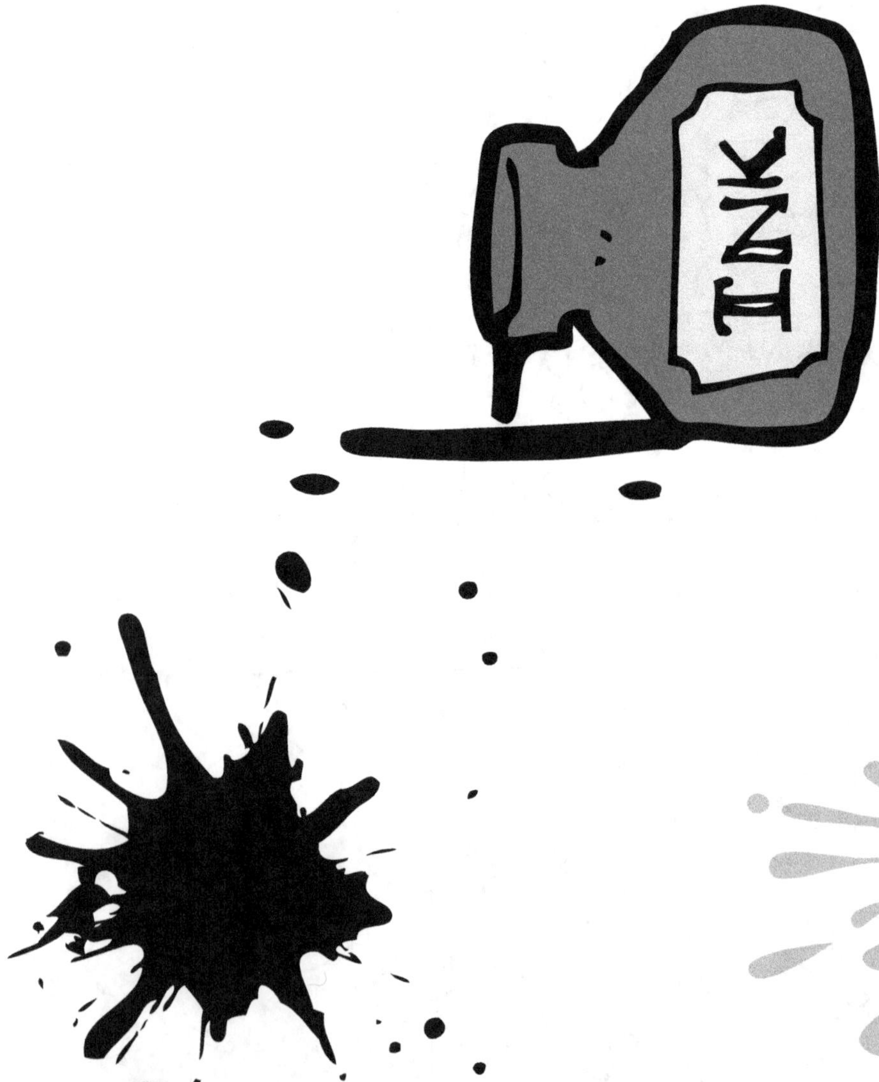